SPORT IN THE AMERICAN WEST
Jorge Iber, Series Editor

EDITORIAL BOARD

Mark Dyreson, Pennsylvania State University

Sarah K. Fields, Ohio State University

Michael E. Lomax, University of Iowa

Samuel O. Regalado, California State University, Stanislaus

Maureen M. Smith, California State University, Sacramento

William E. Tydeman, Texas Tech University

Examining the impact of sport throughout the American West, the series takes on the hard questions. In particular it seeks to illuminate how sport intersects historically with such cultural issues as race, ethnicity, gender, and class. By bringing engaging stories into sharper focus through little-examined or recovered sources, the series aims to engage and enlighten a wide-ranging fan base.

ALSO IN THE SPORT IN THE AMERICAN WEST SERIES

Playing in Shadows by Rob Fink

OUR WHITE BOY

THE LINEUP OF THE WICHITA FALLS/GRAHAM STARS
Manager: Mr. Carl Sedberry, Jr.

Clarence "Rabbit" Myles
(Substitute) James Campbell
(Season 2) Tony Clark

Hubert "Bo" Beasley

Bobby Lee Herron

Emmitt Johnson

Earnest "Fat" Locke

(LHP) T. J. Hawkins
(RHP) Sam "Bam" Brown
(RHP) Jerry Craft

Vernon "Puddin" Higgins
(Season 2) Monroe "Mo" Henderson

Wayne Fisher

(Season 1) Alfred Ray
(Season 2) Emmitt Johnson
(Reserve) "Toothless" Tommy Jones

OUR WHITE BOY

Jerry Craft with Kathleen Sullivan

Foreword by Larry Lester

Texas Tech University Press

This book is typeset in Melior. The paper used in this book meets the
minimum requirements of ANSI/NISO Z39.48–1992 (R1997). ∞

Designed by Kasey McBeath

Library of Congress Cataloging-in-Publication Data
Craft, Jerry, 1937–
Our white boy / Jerry Craft with Kathleen Sullivan ; foreword by Larry Lester.
p. cm. — (Sport in the American West)
Includes bibliographical references and index.
Summary: "Tells the story of Jerry Craft, rancher and former mayor of
Jacksboro, Texas, who was the first white man to play in the West Texas
Colored League during the summers of 1959 and 1960. Craft was pitcher for
the Wichita Falls/Graham Stars, a small, semi-professional, all-black team"
—Provided by publisher.
ISBN 978-0-89672-674-1 (hardcover : alk. paper) 1. Craft, Jerry, 1937–
2. Pitchers (Baseball)—Texas, West—Biography. 3. Baseball players—Texas,
West—Biography. 4. Mayors—Texas—Jacksboro—Biography. 5. Negro
leagues—Texas, West—History. 6. African American baseball players—Texas,
West—History. 7. Baseball—Texas, West—History. 8. Texas, West—Race
relations. I. Sullivan, Kathleen, 1969– II. Title.
GV865.C678C73 2010
796.357092—dc22
[B]   2009046591

Printed in the United States of America
10 11 12 13 14 15 16 17 18 / 9 8 7 6 5 4 3 2 1

Texas Tech University Press
Box 41037 | Lubbock, Texas 79409–1037 USA
800.832.4042 | ttup@ttu.edu | www.ttup.ttu.edu

Author's Note

One of the difficulties of writing a memoir is always the task of substantiation, of holding memory up to scrutiny. Although Kathleen Sullivan and I have held each other's feet to the fire, checking and rechecking, a couple of questions remain open. The first is the name of the league to which the Wichita Falls/Graham Stars belonged. Nowhere does it seem to be documented, but because the Stars and all the other teams and players we competed against knew it only as the West Texas Colored League, that is how I refer to it. The other question is our status: were we truly semi-professional, or were we amateur? As certainly as it never happened, there was always the prospect of divvying up any proceeds that exceeded our expenses. And as certainly as we never made money, those of us who saw such a future played as though we were headed to pro ball. The truth, I suspect, is that the Stars and the League were always a mixture of those on their way up and on their way down. Black or white, semi-professional teams in the fifties were almost always a hybrid, a mixture of those who hoped to earn and those who needed to protect their amateur status. I counted myself among those Stars who saw their standing as semi-professional.

JC

Contents

ILLUSTRATIONS (following page 128)

The 1999 Southwestern Bell African American History Month
Family Day and Negro League Baseball Reunion (Southwest)

Jacksboro's Old Town Team, circa 1931

Jerry Craft's thirteenth birthday party in 1950

Jerry Craft in 1953 on the Jacksboro High School football team

Jim Boley, Bobby Murray, and Jerry Craft, tri-captains
of the 1954 Jacksboro High School football team

J. D. Craft, center, winning a cutting horse championship in 1955

Jerry Craft's high school graduation photo in 1955

Monroe "Mo" Henderson fielding a baseball as
Texas Tech shortstop in 1957

The 1959–60 All-College Football Champions of
Texas Tech University, Sigma Alpha Epsilon Fraternity

Jerry Craft representing his cable television business partner and
Texas State Senator Tom Creighton in Newport, Texas, in 1965

Illustrations

Series Editor's Preface

In the fall of 1992, as an aspiring historian, I entered graduate studies at the University of Utah. Intent on the social history of Latinos/as in the American West, I was sure I'd grasped the proper turf of my chosen discipline—grassroots movements, politics, gender issues, labor, business, military campaigns, and the like. The fundamentals, right? I was focused. Yet over and over I heard about the courses Professor Larry Gerlach was offering in sport history. Certainly I'd read books about baseball and football history, but most were written by newspaper reporters who'd spun anecdotes from their beats into sustained entertainment for confirmed aficionados. The aspect of sport history as serious endeavor seemed a stretch. What was there to learn, beyond the anecdotes, beyond batting averages and team records? More important to a struggling graduate student, could there actually be a tenure-track job at the end of such a course of study?

Curiosity got the better of me, and I visited Dr. Gerlach, who gladly opened my eyes to key topics and themes that stood to illuminate so many aspects of American history, not least of which were issues of race, gender, and class. Sadly, my degree plan left no room for one of Dr. Gerlach's classes, but from that day, mentor and pupil touched base often to talk sports, and my appreciation grew.

Eventually my academic journey led me to Texas Tech University, where I met Professor James Harper. Soon after my arrival, Jim told me about a Mexican American running back, Bobby Cavazos, who had been instrumental in bringing recognition to Texas Tech in the early 1950s. He thought it might be wise for me to research Cavazos's career. I took Jim's advice. The effort generated two articles in historical journals, important currency for assistant professors with a newly minted Ph.D. More than that, it raised questions that led me to a more serious pursuit of sport history. By this time, I'd read books and articles by Allen Guttmann, C. L. R. James, Gerald Gems, Stephen Riess, Gary Mormino, and others—all noted scholars focusing on the intersection of sport and ethnicity/race. Happily I discovered the *Journal of Sport History*, joined the North American Society for Sport History (NASSH), and, most important, read Samuel O. Regalado's book *Viva Baseball! Latin Major Leaguers and Their Special Hunger*. Clearly sport had become a vibrant field of academic inquiry, but too little had been done on the role of Latinos/as. My principal academic question became this: What relevance did the findings of other sport historians hold for the Latino/a experience? Deciding to go all in, I refocused my research agenda—a choice I've never regretted. It has taken me on a fascinating journey among pioneering and heroic teams and individuals and helped open a new vein of inquiry for other scholars of Latino/a and Chicano/a history.

Given my academic emphasis over the past few years, the series editorship of Sport in the American West is a welcome, if daunting, opportunity. The project's goal is ambitious: to examine the impact of sport on American society. Some of the works in the series will be more academic in focus; others, popular including memoir (such as this first work) or even fiction. No matter the bent or category, our objective is to bring into sharper focus how sport intersects with a broad range of issues in American history: race, ethnicity, gender, class, and so forth. It is our sincere expectation that readers will be as entertained as they are enlightened about fundamental societal questions and concerns.

Considering such aspirations, it is a pleasure to introduce Sport in the American West with *Our White Boy* by Jerry Craft with Kathleen Sullivan. Over the past few decades, a substantial number of works have addressed the history of individual players and teams of the Negro Leagues. More recently, studies by scholars such as Michael Lomax and Adrian Burgos have shed light upon tangential topics such as the management of Negro League franchises and the presence of dark-skinned (mostly Cuban) Latinos on team rosters. Bruce Adelson's excellent 1999 study, *Brushing Back Jim Crow: The Integration of Minor League Baseball in the American South*, provides an incisive overview of how a myriad of "Jackie Robinsons," playing in lower levels of professional baseball, broke down barriers of race in the heart of segregated Dixie.

Although there has been extensive work on African Americans participating in our national pastime as professionals or amateurs, little has been done on Caucasians who played on African American squads. One example is the 1998 article by Larry Gerlach, my mentor, entitled "Baseball's Other 'Great Experiment': Eddie Klep and the Integration of the Negro Leagues," which recounts the circumstances by which a white man wound up playing for the Cleveland Buckeyes. To this interesting and historically significant tale, we now add the story of Jerry Craft and his time with the Wichita Falls/Graham Stars in the West Texas Colored League.

The tale of Craft's two seasons (1959 and 1960) with the Stars most assuredly complicates the history of West Texas. Readers will certainly find some of what they can stereotypically expect during this era of American history; Craft's interracial friendships met with surprise from some and outright hostility from others. What readers might not expect, however, lies at the very heart of *Our White Boy*. Craft's moving tribute to men who played for the simple love of the game reveals the power and potential of sport to challenge boundaries, forge friendship, and reshape society. It is this critical accomplishment, which Craft and Sullivan elucidate so elegantly, that makes this work a splendid addition to the collection of anyone who wants to learn more, and think profoundly, about the history of the Lone Star State. Enjoy and look forward to much, much more!

JORGE IBER

Lubbock 2010

FOREWORD

"Next to religion, baseball has furnished a greater impact on American life than any other institution," boasted President Herbert Hoover.

Baseball is our national pastime, our beloved game of cotton candy, hot dogs, salty peanuts, and stale Cracker Jack. Baseball is a rookie with a lump in his throat and sweat on his brow. Baseball is a veteran with a wad of tobacco bulging from his cheek and talking trash. This is America's game! Yes, the all-American game where the only race that matters is the race to the plate. Where color is merely a means to distinguish one team's jersey from that of another team's. Where separation can only be seen on the scoreboard.

However, the time of Jerry Craft's playing days was a time

when racist spikes penetrated the national pastime. A time when black and white players integrated the ball diamond, but not the fans in the grandstands, as America was numb toward the progressive ideals of "mixing."

Our White Boy is more than a story about a young man's dream to play baseball, albeit with a black team in West Texas. Craft offers a stunning portrait of black and white with vivid images of hatred, love, and cautionary boldness. Throughout his journey he exhibited enormous self-control, intellectual fortitude, and spiritual strength in addressing his new environment. This is a groundbreaking and engrossing narrative that may shame some and may expose many of our inner thoughts and beliefs about racism and classism. It is also a story about our social values and our country's deep-rooted obsession with superiority and resistance to social changes. As documented, our national pastime has a lengthy obedience to segregation and discrimination practices. This book historically validates what the great French historian Jacques Barzun once wrote: "Whoever wants to know the heart and mind of America had better learn baseball, the rules and realities of the game." After reading *Our White Boy*, I find Barzun to be Nostradamusly brilliant.

Craft, a visionary from Jacksboro, Texas, who initially didn't know "jack" about the impact his journey would have on his family, friends, and fans of the game, challenged the status quo. His unconditional love of baseball and of people conquered hate across the Lone Star State and beyond.

The future mayor of Jacksboro was the first white fellow to play semi-professional baseball in the West Texas Colored League. At the time, Texans were not ready to accept integration, and Craft was not mentally equipped to deal with the challenges ahead as he fought to overcome prejudice on and off the field. Between dairy and beer breaks, developing fellowship with the fellows was an ongoing, life-changing experience. For two dollars, any Texan could see this vanilla drop in a sea of chocolate pitch like the mound master he was. Batters, both black and white, were often victimized by his dropping curve ball and sneaky fastball. Outs and hits had no color on the scoreboard.

His social indoctrination to baseball started in 1959, before the Voting Rights Act of 1960 and before the 1963 March on Washington. It was the same year when the Boston Red Sox became the last major-league team to integrate by signing Elijah "Pumpsie" Green. Jackie Robinson had crossed the imaginary but real color line and started to break down social and racial barriers with his Brooklyn Dodgers debut in 1947. When he retired in 1957, three major-league teams still had not reserved a locker in their clubhouse for a black player: the Philadelphia Phillies, the Detroit Tigers, and the Red Sox. Although baseball, football, and basketball were some of the first major institutions to integrate, it took parts of America more time to fully embrace the idea. Major League Baseball had followed the operative words from the 1954 Supreme Court decision of *Brown v. Board of Education of Topeka*, to integrate public schools with the mantra of "with all deliberate speed." Fully translated to mean, "Whenever we exhaust all legal remedies and get around to it!" Yes, tortoise-like changes were the norm in the 1950s and 1960s, slowly propelling this country toward a civil rights movement.

Life is not without its challenges and consequences. Craft, in becoming a star athlete, had to overcome an eye injury from an encounter with a bale of hay. As the second best athlete in his family, he became a semi-pro baseball player against his father's wishes, meanwhile confronting his father's fears that he would be drawn away by the world he would discover outside of Jacksboro and Wichita Falls. Despite initial doubts, Craft eventually learned the hard-core traditions of the South from his black teammates and manager Sedberry, and experienced them firsthand. While the Stars often wore mismatched jerseys, they proudly sported matching patches of resilience against hatred, as they turned obstacles into opportunities on enemy ball fields. The team exhibited amazing tenacity in the face of adversity.

Here one will discover Craft's favorite type of glove and bat, his "out" pitch, stories from his formative college days, and the clandestine culinary cow delicacy that transformed him into a power hitter. At times, to Craft's surprise, his outstanding play on the field transcended the racist paradigm and ignited approval from fans of both races, who applauded the skill of his craft with color-blind approval.

The games were full of country hick humor and verbal attacks on ancestry, as semi-pro baseball in Texas was a combination of athletic potential on display, family fun, a little rule-bending, and challenging "who is really in charge here?" Local town teams brought families together, creating social interactions and opportunities to eat, drink, and gamble freely. This came at a time when activities and institutions in the oil and gas state were still segregated, even after death . . . in cemeteries. James Crow, Esquire, was still "king" in Texas, as the Civil Rights Movement was putting on its marching shoes and as the foot soldiers from Wichita Falls traveled to each diamond battlefield. In essence, they became part of the Civil Rights Movement before there was a movement.

Overcoming the social atrocities of the time, Craft became close friends with manager Sedberry and teammates Fat and

Rabbit, as they visited backwoods towns, at times fearing for their lives. The exchange of banter and wisdom between the Stars and other teams teased their innermost thoughts about racism and segregation, historically bound by law, tradition, and geography. These giants embraced the wisdom of Irish philosopher Edmund Burke, who said, "The only thing necessary for evil to triumph is for good men to do nothing."

Craft's trials and tribulations had an impact not only on his beliefs but also on his father's behavior and attitude. Change can be frightening and traumatic, especially if it's not change you have been spoon-fed to accept. Craft paints his father as the poster boy of stubborn men unwilling to change their ideology toward minorities. After two seasons of play on the black team, he saw changes in his father's irrational position on racism and in the beliefs entrenched in some West Texans, but they were quiet changes!

For someone looking at one's self through the eyes of another, race often becomes a creature defined by one's mind and twisted for its own discriminating purposes. Racism in baseball was not static energy. It transformed itself as it went from town to town, team to team, infecting our beloved game of peanuts and Cracker Jack. However, the saga that unfolds may have initiated attitude changes among some Texans. *Our White Boy* may be the most provocative eyewitness account of true southern racial animosity in Texas sports history during the civil rights era, told from a white man's perspective.

This nonstop, engaging story will make you laugh out loud and perhaps cry in silence. Here Craft weaves stories of adversity, confrontation, triumph, shame, and success that will raise your consciousness, stir your soul, and sometimes put a tear in your eye.

Craft is in a league of his own, and all readers can learn

from his journey. Your heart will be surprised by stories so engrossing they will make you want to turn the pages. So go get your Cracker Jack and sit back and enjoy *Our White Boy*. It is truly an American story.

LARRY LESTER
Co-chairman of the Negro Leagues
Committee for the Society for American Baseball Research

ACKNOWLEDGMENTS

Hollace Weiner of the *Fort Worth Star-Telegram*, Bryan Wool-ley of the *Dallas Morning News*, and John Pronk of Channel 8 (WFAA-TV) in Dallas insisted that I revive my 1959 and 1960 seasons with the Wichita Falls/Graham Stars. Thank you for starting me on my journey to find my old teammates.

I would also like to acknowledge my Stars teammates. In the two seasons we toured together, I learned much from them because although they were ordinary men, they were great athletes, and they allowed me to see a world I did not know existed.

Mr. Carl Sedberry, Jr., and Clarence Myles, however, were exceptional. They were extraordinary people, and I hope they learned a little from me.

Although my mother and father did not support my playing with a black team, they supported me with their love and encouraged me to excel in the game of life.

I owe a great deal to Larry McMurtry and Dianne Osanna, who wrote a screenplay version of my story and encouraged me to write a book about my experiences. Larry wouldn't write a book about the Stars because he had too many projects of his own that he wanted to pursue. He didn't understand or particularly like baseball but thought my story needed telling.

After I read Larry and Diana's screenplay, I told them, "This is not a baseball story. Your screenplay is about my growing up on a ranch and my experiences in a small West Texas town."

"No movie is totally a sports movie," Larry told me. "There must be other elements to hold the audience's interest, like romance, conflict, and resolution."

In other words, there was a screenplay, but the book project wasn't going anywhere.

I then called Kathleen Sullivan after seeing an article about her in the *Fort Worth Star-Telegram*. She was teaching sport literature at the University of Texas at Arlington. I thought she might be interested in my story, and she was. She invited me to speak to her classes, and after my lecture she asked me why I had not yet written a book. I told her that Larry wasn't interested in writing a book about baseball, and she said, "I'll help you write that book."

And she has. I found her to be a master at organizing the chapters and their content. Without her professionalism and friendship, this book would never have been written.

Finally, I acknowledge my wife, Pamela, who encouraged me to write what she has also considered an important story involving sports and lasting friendships.

Women have a way of sizing up other women. After meeting Kathleen, Pamela told me, "She's the one to help you do this. Go with her." As usual, Pamela was right.

JERRY CRAFT

Thank you to Jerry Craft. This is your story, and I will always be honored you chose to share it with me. I hope you, your wife, Pamela, your children, and your grandchildren enjoy it.

My father, Pat Sullivan, again served as a fabulous research assistant, editor, golfing buddy, and fellow baseball fan. Dad, we finally saw a Texas team in the World Series. Now we need to see the right one.

My mother, Norma Sullivan Hawkins, provided the emotional support I needed to survive another book project. I love you. This one is for you and Connor.

Connor, you again made me leave the computer long enough to play with you; take you to school, piano lessons, baseball games, swim lessons, soccer practice, and drama camp; and to read books to you. Thanks, sweetie, for helping me have fun.

My grandmother, Margaret "Nonnie" Neptune Sullivan, laughed at several of Jerry's stories. She is not really a baseball fan, but she is a fine golfer. I'm glad that after ninety-three years she can still laugh. Now I'm waiting for her to shoot her age.

Family members who always cheer for me include Jane Sullivan; David "Poppie" Hawkins; Tom, Patrick, Savannah, and Sera Sullivan; Sue and Tom Johnson; Mary Johnson; and Amy and Sean Hughes.

Thank you to all my friends, especially Paula Luna, Karen Foreman, Sue Ooten, Sebastian Francis, Chris and Rania Combs, Jane Schneider, Shana Cannon, Jodie Morris,

Tim Morris, Mark Stamm, David Owens, and Perry and Melissa Harmon, and to the memory of John and Lorraine Lamb.

Many thanks to Larry Lester for his encouragement and for sharing his photographs with us, and to Texas Tech University Press, especially Judith Keeling, Barbara Brannon, Joanna Conrad, Jada Von-Tungeln, Karen Medlin, Emily Sorrells, and Katherine Hinkebein for their unwavering support of Jerry and his story.

Finally, to Johnny and Christopher Stephens, Connor and I are overjoyed to have you on our home team. We love you.

KATHLEEN SULLIVAN

Introduction

As I sat at my desk one afternoon in April 2005, door closed, trying to grade papers, the phone rang.

"I'm Jerry Craft," an older man with a Texas accent said. "I read about you in the *Fort Worth Star-Telegram*. Do you teach baseball literature?"

"Yes, sir," I said.

"I have a baseball story that might be interesting to you," he said.

"OK, shoot," I said. He began telling me that he was the first white guy to play semi-professional baseball in the West Texas Colored League during the summers of 1959 and 1960. He had been a pitcher for the Wichita Falls/Graham Stars, and I could tell that his experiences with an all-black baseball team were very meaningful to him even after nearly fifty years.

His stories were also relevant to the students of an upper-level American literature course I was teaching that spring, English 3300, "Baseball and Film." We were reading six novels that had been adapted to film, including William Brashler's very fine *The Bingo Long Traveling All-Stars and Motor Kings* (1973), which recounts the adventures of a fictitious Negro League team and their leader, Bingo Long. His team takes control of its own finances, abandons the league, and barnstorms the country. The eponymous film version (1976) is worth seeing, especially for performances by James Earl Jones, Richard Pryor, and Billy Dee Williams, but it's not a great film. My syllabus included scenes from it, but now I had a perfect guest lecturer, a real person who had experienced Negro League baseball.

"Mr. Craft, would you please talk to my students?" I asked him.

"Well, I've never spoken to college students, and please call me Jerry," he said.

I persuaded Jerry to travel to Arlington, which is about a two-hour drive from Jacksboro. On the day of his guest lecture, Jerry arrived smartly dressed in a brown sport coat and tie, carrying framed pictures of himself and his teammates during a Negro League reunion and a draft of the screenplay he and Larry McMurtry had been writing. I was impressed. So were my students.

They sat riveted for fifty minutes, and I kicked myself for not recording his presentation. Jerry worried afterward that few asked questions. I explained to him that they were in awe of him and his stories.

After class I asked him why he hadn't written a book. "I

wouldn't know how to do that," he said. "But I'd like to."

I jumped at the chance. "I can help you," I said. I knew that if I recorded his stories, I could organize and edit them into a great book. I would be his ghostwriter and preserve his voice, a white West Texas rancher who loved baseball and fondly recalled his experiences with an all-black baseball team.

By May 2005 we had an outline, and by June he was writing chapter 1. The chapters arrived by U.S. mail, one by one, sometimes with revisions of previous chapters, sometimes alone, all handwritten on long yellow legal pads. The photocopied pages had a few words cut off in the margins. When I asked him to tell me what those words were, he graciously responded with the original chapters.

It's been a joyful collaboration. A few times Jerry identified places in the draft where my imagination had taken over and left his story behind. He would say, "No, it didn't happen this way," and we would talk about it until I got it right. Such is the world of creative nonfiction.

We struggled with the title of the book until Jerry suggested *Our White Boy*. When Jerry joined the Stars, his teammates initially disliked him, calling him "white boy" or simply "boy," but as they grew to know Jerry, they added "our." The name became a term of endearment because they were friends as well as teammates. Jerry became *their* white boy and a full-fledged member of the Stars.

I hope that this book makes Jerry a star again. His friendships with his teammates were unique in Texas, which was still very segregated in the late 1950s and early 1960s. Those friendships later enabled Jerry to serve a diverse constituency and to see their points of view when he entered political life.

Jerry has told me many times that he didn't realize how significant the summers of 1959 and 1960 would be to him later in life. I think in some ways he considers that a character flaw, but I don't. Now, here's Jerry's story as he told it to me.

KATHLEEN SULLIVAN

OUR WHITE BOY

ONE
An Interesting Experiment

N A SWELTERING SUNDAY AFTERNOON in May 1959, while
I was a student on summer break from Texas Tech
University, I pitched my first game for the Wichita
Falls/Graham Stars, a semi-professional all-black
baseball team in the West Texas Colored League. The league
formed in 1953 and included the Stars and six other black
semi-pro teams: the Abilene Blues, the Haskell Yellow Dogs,
the Waco Tigers, the Hamlin Pied Pipers, a team of black soldiers from the Fort Wolters Helicopter Base in Mineral Wells,
and the Zebras from Grandfield, Oklahoma. The Stars played
approximately thirty games during a regular season, which
lasted from April until September.

We also played numerous independent black, white, and
Hispanic teams in the area. The independent black teams
were the Stamford Bulldogs, the Aspermont Hornets, the

Oklahoma City Braves, the Anna Coyotes, the St. Augustine Wolves, and the Abilene Bears. We faced all-white teams from Bowie (the Jackrabbits) and Windthorst (the Trojans). Fort Wolters had segregated teams at that time, so when we traveled to Mineral Wells, we made arrangements to play both teams. The two Fort Wolters teams wore the same uniforms, gray with "Fort Wolters" in black letters across the front, but the black team played much better baseball. Sheppard Air Force Base in Wichita Falls fielded an all-white team, but had no black team. The all-Hispanic teams we played in the area were the Wichita Falls Lobos and the Eastland Hombres.

When the Stars played at home, we always provided our own game officials—the umpires at home, first, and third. Most of the home-plate umps were from Wichita Falls. They were good and did not tolerate players questioning their authority. The umpires brought their own equipment, including chest protectors, face masks, and wisk brooms. The officials on first and third were usually from smaller local towns. The quality of their officiating would vary with their experience and how much they had to drink. We paid them out of our entrance fees and from donations we received when we passed the hat for a few additional dollars during the seventh-inning stretch.

Our operating budget was very small because we had few expenses. We charged a $2 admission at the gate for adults, but kids were free. The players' wives sold soft drinks and cooked burgers and hot dogs during the games. Their fundraising efforts never amounted to much. None of us was ever paid, but we accepted small donations from the black community to pay for our baseballs.

Those donations were meaningful to us for a number of

reasons. We could not make a living from playing baseball and therefore could not afford to spend what little money we had on baseball equipment. We enjoyed playing the game, and we were happy to do it, but we all worked during the week and sometimes on weekends at our regular jobs. In fact, our team's finances were similar to the finances of other black semi-professional teams around us. According to Texas baseball historian Robert Fink, our inability to support ourselves through baseball and our need to have regular jobs was the "one characteristic that united semi-professional black baseball and distinguished it from professional African American baseball" (2007).

During my time with the league, our teams were loosely organized. We traveled in whatever cars were running to games that took place only if enough players arrived by game time. Some of our players were more reliable than others, and most tried their best to play baseball around work schedules and family commitments. None of us was under contract with any major-league teams or their farm clubs.

Some West Texas Colored League teams rarely played each other because of the great distances between their towns in West and Central Texas and in Oklahoma. Two hundred miles separate Wichita Falls and Waco, and such Texas-sized road trips were costly. We could barely afford to travel to regular-season away games in Waco, which meant a playoff schedule was not in our budgets. I also had to return to school at Texas Tech in the fall after my first summer with the Stars, making me unavailable for playoff games even if we could afford them. Although we never crowned an official champion, all of the teams we played were very aware of our record against them.

During my time with the Stars, only our manager Mr.

Sedberry kept a scorebook of our games for his personal use, and our league standings received no media attention. My memories and the recollections of my surviving teammates, Clarence "Rabbit" Myles and Monroe "Mo" Henderson, together with a few interviews we've given and an unpublished interview with Mr. Sedberry, form the sparse record we have of our time together. Notably, the history of many Negro baseball leagues "remains incomplete because of the paucity of written accounts, incomplete box scores, and a general failure on the part of black baseball management and journalists alike to provide a historical record for the most statistically conscious of all sports" (Cottrell 2001). The West Texas Colored League never appeared in either of the two Wichita Falls newspapers, *The Wichita Falls Times Record News* and *The Wichita Daily Times,* in the 1950s and 1960s. Both covered Major League Baseball extensively and regularly reported scores from teams in the local Oil Belt League, the Texas League, and the collegiate Southwest Conference. No Stars scores, however, were ever reported. We were simply too informal of a league to be included on a sports page.

The two African American newspapers published in Dallas at that time, *The Dallas Express* and *The Dallas Star Post*, included baseball reports as part of their weekly coverage of the area. In the spring each reported high school and college baseball scores, stories about the Negro American League, and features on black baseball players who were playing Major League Baseball, but the semi-professional West Texas Colored League wasn't mentioned. Black newspapers decreased their coverage of black teams when Jackie Robinson began playing for the Brooklyn Dodgers in 1947 and when Larry Doby followed in the American League in 1948. In the late 1940s, "the black newspapers continued to write of the exploits of black major leaguers, while ignoring the all-black teams" (Fink 2007). By 1960 the *Express* paid greater attention to San Francisco Giant Willie Mays and his teammate Willie McCovey, who had won Rookie of the Year honors in 1959, than to the local black teams.

Despite this trend, in 1959–60 the *Express* and the *Star Post* followed the Dallas Negro Baseball Association, a city-wide baseball league, and its defending champions, the Texas Road Runners. The Road Runners were such a strong team that by May 1959 their record was already 12–1. According to a May 16, 1959, *Star Post* article, the Road Runners "whipped an all-white Fort Worth team 14–4 last Wednesday night." Apparently, the rivalry between Dallas and Fort Worth extended into contests between their black and white baseball teams.

Segregated baseball has a long history in Texas, including the teams of the Texas Negro League that played in the 1920s followed by the all-black teams of the Texas-Oklahoma-Louisiana (TOL) League from 1929 to 1932. At different times those teams played in the same cities as the white Texas League: Shreveport, Dallas, Houston, Tulsa, San Antonio, Oklahoma City, Wichita Falls, and Fort Worth. The TOL teams used the Texas League's fields when the white teams were playing away games (Presswood and Holaday 2004). Dallas was home to the Black Giants, but the other TOL names often shadowed the names of their associated Texas League teams, such as the Fort Worth Black Panthers and the white Fort Worth Cats.

After decades of blacks and whites playing on separate teams in the Dallas–Fort Worth area, the visionary owner of the white Dallas Eagles, Dick Burnett, decided to integrate the Texas League. He made a startling preseason announcement in 1952, calling for black and white players to share Burnett Field in Oak Cliff. On April 13, 1952, the Dallas Eagles' first black player, pitcher Dave Hoskins, took the mound. His performance was greeted with great enthusiasm by Dallas's black community, though Hoskins's fans were still watching him from segregated seats. Burnett's bold move and Hoskins's 22–10 record for the 1952 season encouraged the Texas League's San Antonio team to integrate in 1953 (Holaday and Presswood 2004). The Fort Worth Cats followed in 1955 with the addition of Maury Wills and Eddie Moore (Presswood and Holaday 2004).

These events did not make an impression on my Stars teammates. They didn't follow the teams in Dallas or read *The Dallas Express* and *The Dallas Star Post*. Instead, the Stars simply played baseball and enjoyed the companionship of their teammates and rivals. When I joined them, I realized that our time together on the field meant more to us than receiving newspaper coverage.

While the press ignored us, we were busy facing each team at least twice every summer, usually for one game at home and another game away. Some teams were fun to play, like the Haskell Yellow Dogs, and we tried to play them as often as possible. We enjoyed postgame food, refreshments, and fellowship with them at the Yellow Dog Tavern west of Haskell. When we played at home, we scheduled our games on Sunday afternoons at Spudder Park in Wichita Falls and on Wednesdays at the Graham Public Baseball Field in Graham, a town about sixty miles south of Wichita Falls. The Stars, Hispanic, and white baseball teams reserved game times through the Wichita Falls recreation department. The first game started at 1:00 p.m., the last about 8:00 p.m.

The Stars' summer schedule in 1959 and 1960 included home games in Wichita Falls and in Graham, and during both summers we also played a tournament in Ranger, Texas, held on the Juneteenth holiday weekend, when the players were given time off from work. Summers and holidays meant that the teams of the league entertained their fans with all-black baseball—until the day I joined the Stars, that is, making it the first and only team in the league to integrate.

When I initially took the mound for the Stars, I had not thrown a baseball to a black person since my sandlot days in my hometown of Jacksboro, Texas. There, despite the segregation in every other part of life, our childhood games had involved all the children in town. My white grade-school friends and I never questioned why we played baseball with black children but did not go to their schools or churches, eat in their restaurants, or even drink from their water fountains.

The integration of the Stars is more meaningful to me now than it was in 1959. Back then, I was just happy to play baseball. Now I realize the significance of our achievement. It was not initiated by local politicians, national legislation, or Supreme Court precedent. Instead, Mr. Carl Sedberry, Jr., the Stars' manager, simply invited me to play because the team needed good pitching to win, and the Stars loved winning games. Pitching was hard to find in West Texas, and I was a very good (albeit white) veteran pitcher who was available.

The Stars and I were not making a moral or ethical statement, though I suppose it was one, in its own time and way. When Mr. Sedberry invited me to try out for the team, he mentioned paying me, so I initially thought that playing baseball with the Stars would be a great part-time job for a college student on summer break. Few opportunities existed to make money in West Texas, except on the oil rigs and cattle ranches, far more dangerous and dirty work than playing baseball. My traditional summer job had always been working long hours for my father on our family's cattle ranch. A chance to make money playing the game I loved would be an unexpected bonus that summer. In other words, at first I thought I would do it for the money, but I was never paid. I started to ask Mr. Sedberry a time or two about my paycheck, but I quickly realized the meager funds we collected would not allow my team to pay me.

Mr. Sedberry later admitted to me that he knowingly misled me about pay to entice me to pitch that first game. He said, "Really, we couldn't afford to pay you, but we sure could try!" I think he also knew that once I pitched for them and we started winning games, I would have too much fun to worry about a paycheck.

What became more important to me than a salary was developing an enjoyment, appreciation, and respect for the Stars. This is the story of our time together.

My journey with the Stars began the same day I returned home after completing my fourth year of college, but I had not yet graduated. I had few plans for the summer except working on my father's ranch and visiting with friends before going back to Lubbock for my fifth year of school. I also planned to play semi-pro baseball that summer, but I did not know what teams still existed in the area. With the advent of televised major-league baseball, local players seemed less interested in playing our national pastime than in watching it on television, and, consequently, many of our local teams had folded.

In 1959 I was twenty-two years old, a 6'2", 185-pound West Texas ranch boy with green eyes and short, wavy, dark brown hair. Everyone at that time wore flat-top haircuts, with hair sticking up all over, shaved evenly across the top. No matter how hard I tried, my hair would not stand up, even when I used a sticky pomade. As much as I hated it then, I sure wish I had that head of hair now. I also had an easygoing personality, but I was always a little self-conscious of my irregularly shaped left pupil, a result of a childhood accident.

When I was nine years old, I received my first pocket knife for Christmas, the same kind of knife my hero Red Rider used during the twenty-five-cent Saturday afternoon matinees I saw at the Jack and the Mecca theatres in Jacksboro. I watched in awe as Red threw his knife into a bale of cotton, which must have impressed the outlaw standing next to it because he took his hand away from his holster and retreated. I decided to practice the same move with my own knife.

We did not have any cotton at my house, so I found a bale of hay, propped it against a tree, and threw my knife. The knife hit the tree, bounced back, and lodged in my left eye. I was in pain, but I also knew I was in trouble. I went inside, where my mother was concentrating on her Christmas present, a Singer sewing machine. Her back was to me when I told her, "Mom, I have a knife stuck in my eye."

"Um-humm," she replied as she continued sewing.

"Mom, I really do," I said.

She turned around, stood up, and fell on the floor. The doctors did their best, taping my head tightly to close the wound in my eye. When it healed, they wanted me to wear glasses, but my father would not allow it.

"I want my son to be a very good athlete," he told them. "He can't wear glasses. He will have to adjust."

I did. As a ten-year-old pitcher on the sandlot in Jacksboro, I modified my stretch so that I could check the runner on first base. I couldn't see the base runners as easily as I once had, so I compensated by turning my head. That allowed me to see the runners, especially one on first base, with my right eye. This exaggerated head turn might be penalized under today's rules because home-plate umpires could interpret this motion as part of my delivery. If I didn't deliver a pitch after turning my head, the umpire could call a balk and allow the runners on base to advance.

My eyesight also changed other aspects of my game. As a batter, I learned to turn my head farther to the left so my right eye could catch the rotation of the pitched ball. When I fielded, I also turned my head so that I could catch fly balls and throws from other players. I have never considered my eyesight a handicap, though I often think of that foolish afternoon with the villain bale of hay.

On the day I started summer break, I carpooled home from Tech with my friends and dropped them off at their homes. I then drove up the semicircular front drive to my parents' large, two-story white-brick house on Live Oak Street in Jacksboro. I could see my mother through the door of the screened-in back porch that joined her kitchen to the garage. She was eagerly anticipating my return and waved to me. Louise "Lou" Craft was then only forty-five years old, a petite woman at 5'3", who wore her coal-black hair swept into a bun on the back of her head, reminding me of her Cherokee Indian heritage.

I unloaded my suitcases from my brown and white 1955 Ford, entered the back door, and was warmly greeted by my mother and Humpty, a friendly brown and white terrier. My father, J. D. "Jay" Craft had not returned home from Craft Ranch headquarters, which our family still owns, about thirteen miles northeast of Jacksboro.

Over the years Craft Ranches has grown into a sizable cattle business that consists of about four separate ranches in Jack County, covering more than seven thousand acres. We also have operations in Harding and Colfax counties in New

Mexico that total more than twenty-five thousand acres. Then as now, cattle ranching defined our family in many of the same ways baseball did. Ranching was a bond between me and my father, just like baseball was, and I was looking forward to helping him with the family business that summer, though he tended to work a lot harder at ranching than I did. I was still a very young person and more interested in summer fun than work.

As my mother and I waited for my father to return home for dinner, we visited in the kitchen. She updated me on all of our small town's news. A new Methodist preacher had come to town while I was away, and my mother analyzed his strengths and weaknesses, as well as those of his wife. We also talked about how the all-girl semi-pro softball team my sister Linda played for was faring. Finally, my mother reminded me of those who had died and who they were kin to, an important part of retaining our small-town roots and heritage. Her report went something like this: "Sally Jones died two weeks ago. Surely you remember she was Jack Henderson's aunt. You also know that her maiden name was Brumelow and her first husband was a Snook." We still talk like this in Jacksboro, but to a much lesser extent.

I listened attentively while she cooked my favorite supper, chicken-fried steak with cream gravy, French fries, pinto beans, biscuits, cherry cobbler, and iced tea. Although it was only May, my mother's home-grown tomatoes were on the table as well. It was good to be back.

"When are you going to graduate?" she teased me.

"Oh, next year, Mama," I told her.

"Well, you've been at that school since the fall of 1955. Don't you think it's time to graduate?" she asked again.

"Yes, ma'am," I said.

I didn't want to discuss it because I didn't want my father to be reminded that I was going to be a fifth-year senior at Texas Tech. Luckily, she changed the topic and told me something that would change my life.

"A man named Sedberry has called a couple of times to talk to you about playing semi-pro baseball for his team this summer. Do you know any Sedberrys?" she asked.

"No, I don't," I told her.

"He said they live in Graham," she added.

"No, I still can't place them," I said.

I wasn't surprised that someone had called about my pitching. I had played semi-professional baseball for Wichita Falls in the Oil Belt League during the previous two summers and earned a good reputation. I told her that I would return the call that afternoon, but before I got the chance Mr. Sedberry called again.

As I was helping my mother set the table for dinner, the phone rang.

"Is this Mr. Jerry Craft?" a voice asked.

"Yes, sir," I replied. My mother raised me to be a southern gentleman, so I added "sir" to any "yes" or "no" question from an elder, especially from someone I didn't know. While my mother may have taught me my manners, my father and his thick western belt had enforced them.

"Are you playing any summer ball right now?"

"No, sir," I said as I was balancing silverware and plates, the phone cord stretched across the table.

"Well, we really want you to play for our team. I'm Mr. Sedberry, the manager." I stopped what I was doing to listen more carefully. Playing baseball for the summer would be a great way to pass the time in my small town before returning to Lubbock.

"Who's your team?"

"The Wichita Falls Stars."

"I never heard of you guys. I thought I knew all the semi-pro teams in the area. Are you a newly formed team?"

"Oh, we've been around a long time. We've got an excellent ball club, but we don't have very good pitching. We need a top-notch pitcher. We watched you play for the Cruise Tire Company last summer in Wichita Falls, and you're exactly who we need. With you we can have the best record in our league."

I enjoyed hearing compliments about my playing, and a summer job would give me some extra money for school expenses in the fall. "Well, what do you pay?" I asked.

"For a pitcher of your class, seventy-five dollars a game," he said.

I was really excited. That would be the most money I'd ever been paid for pitching. I felt I was finally receiving the recognition I deserved as one of the better semi-pro pitchers in the area. "How many games a week?" I asked.

My mother, eyeing me suspiciously as I talked baseball, looked at the clock. She knew my father would be home soon, and she also knew that he expected me to help him on the ranch that summer, not pitch for another baseball team.

"Two games a week," he said. "Wednesday nights and Sunday afternoons."

A hundred and fifty dollars a week would be a very large sum of money for a part-time summer job in 1959, so I immediately agreed. "I'd be happy to try out for your team," I said.

"Meet us this Sunday at Spudder Park in Wichita Falls for a game against our old rivals, the Abilene Blues. By the way, we've never beat them. Play with us and see if you like us, and we'll see if we like you," he said.

"I've never heard of the Abilene Blues either," I said.

"They've been around a long time, too. Come by at two o'clock. I look forward to seeing you."

"Thank you, Mr. Sedberry. I'll be there."

I hung up the phone and shrugged at my mother. "I have no idea who these guys are or how good their team is. We'll look each other over Sunday afternoon. They have the advantage, though, because they saw me play last summer in the Oil Belt League. And they're obviously working people because they only play on Sunday afternoons and Wednesday nights."

She looked doubtful, so I tried to reassure her.

"It's just a tryout," I told her. "And it's only twice a week. I can still work on the ranch. And boy, they must have a sugar daddy for a sponsor because they are going to pay me seventy-five dollars a game to pitch!"

When my father arrived for supper, our conversation immediately turned to ranch news and the weather. Rainfall, or lack of it, controls how many head of cattle we can sell and how profitable they will be.

As I listened to him update me on the family business, I was thinking that my father would probably approve of my playing baseball because he shared my love for the game. He had never cared who I played for in the past, but he preferred I play in Jacksboro so that he could occasionally watch me on Sunday afternoons without having to travel. Our meals together often included discussions of the major-league pennant races and the individual statistics of nearly every player, and we quickly reviewed the major-league standings.

When I finally introduced the idea of my playing baseball that summer and explained how much they would pay me, my father responded with mixed emotions.

"I knew you'd probably want to do it, and on Sundays we only have a few chores," he said. "I wish I knew why they're going to pay you so much money, though."

While my father was very proud of my baseball accomplishments, he would often remind me that I had gone as far as my talents would take me. My father wasn't trying to downplay my talents or chances to play baseball professionally. Instead, he worried about what would happen to the ranch, the land he loved, if I left home to play baseball and saw what else life had to offer. He thought I'd never come back to Jacksboro and the ranch if I saw other parts of the world.

His good friend Otis Henderson shared this concern about his own son, Monroe, who was also my friend. Monroe had been offered a contract to play for the Baltimore Orioles, which caused a lot of gossip around town. No one from Jacksboro had ever played organized baseball, and many of Otis and my father's friends had asked them, "Well, what are you going to do when Monroe and Jerry leave town?"

Such concerns frightened my father. Ranchers are a different breed who have a unique view of their land. Larry McMurtry, who was raised on a ranch in neighboring Archer County, once wrote to me that he views my work as a form of slavery because I'm so bound to my land. Instead, I believe my land is an extension of myself, for which my family sacrificed much to carve out our lives and our homes. They fought, bled, and struggled for it, and when they died they passed it on to their sons. Our ancestors still live on in our land.

My father had accepted, even with some degree of fatalism, his role as a steward of our land, fulfilling that task even though he spent less time with his family. I have tried to balance my work life and family life, but I often feel guilty about leaving the animals when I take trips. However, I always return and experience the joys of successfully pulling a calf from a first-calf heifer, seeing the calf gasp for breath and struggle to its feet, and watching it nurse for the first time. I'm amazed that the heifer immediately knows how to mother her baby.

I love the land and ranching. Unlike my ancestors, however, I went to college, saw some of the world, and had other professional interests and hobbies. When my father was dying, he wanted me to promise that my children would not sell our ranches when I died. I could not make him that promise. All I can do is pass down the land to them in the best condition possible and hope they maintain it. The land will always outlive us.

Despite his skepticism about my potential baseball income, my father finally allowed me to skip my chores on the ranch the Sunday of the Stars tryout because he loved baseball and hoped I'd do well. He had a few chores to do that day, or he might have come to see me play. He had seldom critiqued the games he attended, even when I was the losing pitcher. I think that his silence meant he was impressed and recognized I'd become a better ballplayer than he once was.

He wished me luck, and I started the hourlong drive to Wichita Falls alone. I've always been grateful that he did not travel with me to my tryout with the Stars. I am certain he would not have allowed me to walk onto a field with black baseball players, much less play a game with them. I can picture us returning home in silence and never speaking about that day again.

Luckily, I was by myself as I traveled to Spudder Park, a minor-league baseball park named not for potatoes but after the expression "spudding in an oil well," meaning "drilling a well," from back in the early days of oil production. The field was once the longtime home of the Spudders, who arrived in Wichita Falls in 1920 after local businessman J. Alvin Gardner bought the team and moved it from Waco. In June 1922 the stadium caught fire during a game and burned to the ground but was later rebuilt.

The Spudders won 102 games in 1927 to become the Texas League champions and then won the Dixie Series championship in four straight games against New Orleans. They folded in early 1957, but not before they were a farm team for the Pittsburgh Pirates (1920–21), Chicago Cubs (1922–25), St. Louis Browns (1928–32; 1948–51), Boston/ Milwaukee Braves (1952/1953), and finally the Brooklyn Dodgers (1956–57). Some of the greatest baseball players in the world had appeared between the 325-foot foul poles. In 1930 the Spudders beat the Yankees and Babe Ruth. The crowd of 8,635 fans was delighted to see the Babe hit two towering home runs. The Yankees' Don Larson pitched for the Spudders in 1950 before being called up to New York. Even as late as September 14, 1950, more than 3,300 fans paid to see the Spudders play in the rain.

Spudder Park also held special childhood memories for me as the place where I saw my first major-league game in 1953. The New York Giants played the Cleveland Indians as an overflow crowd stood along the first- and third-base lines down to the outfield fences. Additional chairs and bleachers were set up behind the crowd. I stood about halfway down the left-field line, holding my glove and waiting for a foul ball. Late in the game, a high fly ball came drifting toward me, but just before I could catch it, Giants player Monte Irvin pushed me aside. He made the grab and gave me a menacing look.

I continued to visit Spudder Park often over the years. When I was attending high school, my friends and I discovered Elvis's music on the nickel juke box at the drive-in root beer stand on Live Oak Street in Jacksboro, and we became immediate fans. He performed at Spudder Park on August 22, 1955, and those few of us with cars caravanned from the Jacksboro courthouse to the baseball field. Elvis sang and danced on a temporary stage built between the pitcher's mound and home plate. We danced along with him, making the entire stadium shake beneath our pounding feet. I had also pitched there many times, once in a 1955 bi-district baseball playoff game for Jacksboro High School and during my time in the Oil Belt League.

I arrived in Wichita Falls early for my Stars tryout, about 1:00 p.m. As I pulled into the asphalt parking lot beside the ballpark, midafternoon heat radiated off the pavement, making its tar patches bubble. I got out of my car and walked toward the main entrance. The wooden grandstands, about thirty rows deep, extended down the entire first- and third-base lines. The stands could seat about 2,500 people, all shaded by an overhang that protected them from the Texas sun. Spudder Park was painted a dark green, which provided good visibility for the fielders. The outfield fences wore a complementary shade. By 1959 the facilities had begun to look run down. Paint peeled and long benches sagged from the weight of people and years.

As I walked down the steps that led to the field, I stopped abruptly. The stands on this day held about two hundred black people, all eagerly anticipating a game and trying to stay cool in the intense heat that begins as early as May in West Texas. I looked down on the field, and two teams of all-black players were warming up. In fact, everyone was black.

"Wrong address," I thought and climbed the stadium steps to return to my car. I left Spudder Park and drove to two other small ball parks on the west side of town, Lucy Park and the city's municipal stadium. Both were empty. I was really confused. Because I had no way to contact Mr. Sedberry, I returned to Spudder Park to solve this mystery.

No white people were in sight when I pulled back into the parking lot, so I concluded that the black teams must be playing before the white teams, and, as was often the case, the games were not starting on time. I thought I would wait for the white teams, but I didn't know where to wait for them.

I again got out of my car and walked slowly back down the stadium steps, looking for a white face in the black crowd. I hoped to find someone who could tell me where the white baseball teams were; the game was less than an hour away from starting. As I moved toward the field, a large, well-dressed black man, roughly ten years older than I was, strolled leisurely toward me, hand outstretched, and said, "Mr. Craft? I'm Mr. Sedberry, Carl Sedberry, Jr."

My mouth dropped open. I shook his hand, and he chuckled and said, "Well, Mr. Craft, you didn't know I was black, did you?"

During our phone conversation, I would never have thought to ask him what race he was. I assumed the Stars were a white team. I could never have imagined a black baseball team would call me for a tryout. It simply wasn't done that way at that time.

I slowly shook his hand and carefully considered his appearance. His immaculate blue coat and tie and matching snap-brim hat contrasted sharply with my Cruise Tire Company uniform, off-white with faded black lettering, the same uniform I had worn for the last two summers. I also wore an old drab green rubber warm-up jacket that easily identified me as a pitcher. It was sort of a letter jacket in those days. When I came on the field wearing that jacket, everybody knew I was the gunslinger.

Steel-toe plates were another status symbol pitchers enjoyed at that time. The plates laced up and screwed into our right shoes to keep them from wearing out when we dragged them across the ground after delivering a pitch. I still wore the same shoes from last summer, which added to the contrast between me and Mr. Sedberry in his polished dress shoes.

"Mr. Sedberry?" I said incredulously, still shaking his hand. He nodded and smiled silently, holding my eye steady in his. "No, sir, I didn't know you were black," I said.

"I didn't mention it because I thought if you knew we were a black baseball club you wouldn't want to play with us. Make any difference?" he asked.

"I'm not sure," I replied, honestly.

"Well, are you prejudiced?"

"I don't think so," I said.

"You've played a lot of baseball. Did you ever think about playing for a black baseball team?" he asked.

"No, sir, I've never even seen a black baseball team until today."

He considered me carefully and said, "Well, give us a try, and see if you like us."

"Well, how do you think your team is going to react to me?"

"I don't know. It's going to be an interesting experiment. It may be an interesting season," he said.

"Mr. Sedberry, I don't know if I want to be part of an experiment," I said.

"That's fair," he replied. "We scouted you last summer, and we have word from your hometown that you are not a prejudiced man."

"I don't think I am, but this is not what I was prepared for," I told him.

"Come with me," he said reassuringly.

Mr. Sedberry led me through the players' entrance and onto the field. The stands were suddenly quiet when the fans saw me. I was acutely aware of why I had been invited to play at this particular baseball park. The black baseball teams could use Spudder Park, but other facilities in the area were reserved for white teams only. I wondered if this fact bothered some of the players gathered there.

We moved behind the dugout, where I was greeted by Jacksboro's Alfred Ray, the Stars' catcher. He and I shook hands. I was surprised to see him.

"Alfred scouted you last summer in Wichita Falls and suggested that I recruit you. He's the man who believes you are not prejudiced," explained Mr. Sedberry.

"I'm glad you are willing to play with us today. It's good to see you again," Alfred said.

"Good to see you, too," I told him.

As children, Alfred and I played sports and swam together, and he later told me that I always treated the black children well when we played baseball at Fort Richardson in Jacksboro and in my front yard. He told me he was especially fond of my mother, who brought us snacks when we were taking breaks from the games. He once laughingly told me, "Your mother told me not to tell white people that I liked a white woman so much!"

As we grew older, we had grown apart because we lived in a segregated town. He was now a bear of a man, 6'4" and 225 pounds, always laughing. On the field he was never in a hurry. His size made him a great target behind home plate, and the threat of his tremendous right arm held even the fastest runners on first base.

From where he and I stood, we could see several players throwing baseballs to each other. One was a center fielder I'd never met before, Clarence "Rabbit" Myles, nicknamed for his speed in the outfield. Mr. Sedberry always called Rabbit "Mud Duck" or just "Duck," which I later learned was Rabbit's CB radio handle.

Rabbit was a small man, about 5'6" or 5'7", but very muscular. He was not, at first glance, physically imposing. His gray uniform sported the name of his business across the back, Myles Construction. Rabbit, like me, had started as an outsider to the team because he was not originally from the area. He had grown up in San Antonio and worked construction for H. P. Zachary, but the company relocated him to their Graham office. He decided to make nearby Wichita Falls his permanent home after he met his wife, Arnita, there.

When Rabbit arrived in Wichita Falls, one of the first people he met was Mr. Sedberry. Rabbit happened to see the Stars practicing and stopped for a minute to watch. Mr. Sedberry, an extremely outgoing person, spotted him and asked, "Do you play baseball?"

"Well, yeah, I play baseball," Rabbit said.

"When did you last play?" Mr. Sedberry wanted to know.

"I played some before I finished high school," he said. "I can run, so they would put me in the outfield. Called me 'Rabbit.'"

"Why don't you join us?" Mr. Sedberry asked him.

Rabbit agreed, and soon after he met Earnest "Fat" Locke, Bobby Lee Herron, Emmitt Johnson, and Wayne Fisher. They enjoyed their practices and games. After they finished playing, they would rest under nearby trees and drink beer and soda. The Stars seemed content, but Mr. Sedberry wanted more for his team. He was a competitor and realized that they needed better pitching to win games.

As I walked with Mr. Sedberry toward the field for my tryout, Rabbit was playing catch along the first-base line with right fielder Bobby Lee Herron, a fantastic power hitter. Bobby was physically impressive. He was probably 6'3" or 6'4" and weighed 240 pounds. He exuded haughtiness and wore his old Kansas City Monarchs uniform with pride. I had never seen one before, and I was very impressed.

Both men stopped what they were doing and stared at me. Obviously they had never considered playing baseball with a white man before. I could hear their conversation. Bobby asked Rabbit, "Who the hell is that white boy?"

"Bobby, I bet that is our new pitcher," he said. "I heard Mr. Sedberry say he's a college boy, but he's home for the summer to help his dad. Maybe we can convince him to play with us on Wednesdays and the weekends. We could use some pitching."

"You mean to tell me we are going to play ball with a white boy?" Bobby asked.

"No, Bobby, he is going to play with us," Rabbit answered.

Mr. Sedberry could tell that their conversation made me uncomfortable. He tried to put me at ease. "Now, have a seat, Mr. Craft," he said. I smiled at him as I turned to the dugout. I sat there and watched the rest of the team warm up.

About fifteen minutes later Mr. Sedberry waved me toward him. When I emerged from the dugout, everyone, even the fans in the stands, became quiet and stared at me. He introduced me to the rest of the team as "Mr. Craft." From that day forward, he always called me Mr. Craft, and I always called him Mr. Sedberry, although the other players often called him Carl or Junior, and he used their first names as well.

The Stars had assembled around us, and I was received rather coolly, my white face standing out among the black. We were a mismatched bunch, sporting uniforms of various shades and styles. No two were alike. The team wore an assortment of jerseys and baseball pants in faded grays, light blues, and whites, not one jersey with the lettering "Stars" on either the front or the back. The Stars had all evidently played for other teams in previous seasons and kept their old uniforms or borrowed uniforms for the game. All the pants had mended knees where sliding into base had torn the material, but even the patches did not match the color of the pants. Only Bobby Lee Herron's Monarchs ensemble was not ragged.

My uniform was in good shape, comparatively, and I knew that my teammates probably couldn't afford new uniforms that would only be worn twice a week and damaged repeatedly.

As they approached me, a few of the players nodded vaguely in my direction, if they acknowledged my presence at all. In 1959 Wichita Falls, like most of Texas, was still segregated. Blacks and whites in the area tolerated one another even though they continued to live in different neighborhoods and shop at different stores. The separate drinking fountains I remembered from my childhood had disappeared, but not the racist attitudes that had originally created them. I didn't know if the Stars would accept me on their team. The looks on their faces showed their ambivalence.

The Stars continued to eye me suspiciously while Mr. Sedberry reviewed our game strategy. "Men, you know we've never beaten the Blues, but we will today. They're just a bunch of cocky ballplayers. Now, I think we should start our worst pitcher," Mr. Sedberry said as he slapped a young left-handed pitcher on the back, Sam "Bam" Brown, who was about my age, twenty-two, and much skinnier than I was. I thought he could have used a few servings of my mother's chicken-fried steak and mashed potatoes.

"Yes, sir," Sam said eagerly, agreeing easily with Mr. Sedberry's assessment of his skills. I'd watched Sam struggle through a few of his warm-up pitches, and I knew that I was by far the better pitcher. I couldn't understand why Mr. Sedberry wanted Sam to start the game and not me. Mr. Sedberry continued explaining his plan to us.

"Let them get ahead and overconfident, and then we'll put in the big artillery. We'll blow them back to Abilene!" he shouted.

The Stars cheered, clapped their hands, and headed back to the field to resume their warm-ups.

I sat by Mr. Sedberry in the dugout. "Mr. Sedberry, who's our big artillery?" I asked.

"Why, that's you, baby!" Mr. Sedberry smiled as he glanced at me, a white college boy pitching his first game in a colored league.

"Let me get this straight. We're playing a team we've never beaten, starting our worst pitcher, letting them get ahead, and then putting me in? You're expecting to win this game?" I asked.

"Trust me, Mr. Craft. It's going to work. Like I said, they are cocky and overconfident," he told me.

Such logic bewildered me, but I knew better than to question Mr. Sedberry before my first game on his team. Instead, I looked up into the stands. As I watched the fans, I thought Mr. Sedberry's plan might work. This baseball game was equal parts social event and athletic competition, with the socializing sometimes outweighing the athleticism. Friends visited loudly through each inning, placed bets, and drank beer. They might not notice how bad a pitcher Sam was or how far behind we were when I started pitching.

A few minutes before the start of the game Mr. Sedberry sent me to the bullpen, a dingy area on the far side of the dugout, flat as the West Texas prairie and filled with empty beer bottles. Although I was a sizable athlete, I felt fragile in front of the pleasantly inebriated though boisterous crowd. The group in the bullpen, however, didn't intimidate me. "Toothless" Tommy Jones, the bullpen catcher from Breckenridge, Texas, who was supposed to warm me up, looked old enough to be my grandfather, even older because of his missing teeth. He was probably in his mid-fifties, and I was afraid I'd hurt him.

I waved Mr. Sedberry over. "I don't think he is strong enough to catch me."

"Just throw the ball," Mr. Sedberry replied.

"OK, but I really think I might hurt him," I said.

Mr. Sedberry slowly walked away without another word. He was not in a hurry. Later in the season I would learn that all of his trips to the mound were the same pace as that first trip to visit me in the bullpen. No matter what the situation, Mr. Sedberry took his time. His walk characterized the league, whose games had two start times, late and later. I had no choice but to begin warming up.

After a few easy pitches, I noticed the old catcher was singing to me. He'd rock back and forth and sing these little songs, not a tooth in his head. Tommy hummed, grunted, and groaned his way through blues songs, occasionally punctuated by a soft exclamation of "Oh, Lawdy." He seemed not only old to me, but frail and thin. Soon the tempo of my pitches increased. I got ready to start throwing curves, which all pitchers indicate by flipping their gloved hand over. I said, "I'm going to throw some curves," to the catcher, just to make sure he understood.

"Throw your curves in here, white boy. I'll catch 'em," he replied.

"Yes, sir. But you need to watch out for these curves, sir, because they drop, and they're hard to catch." My curve balls not only broke over the plate but also dropped. Most pitchers at that time threw a flat curve ball that simply moved along the same horizontal plane as it traveled over the plate. Instead, I snapped my wrist downward, which not only produced the spin needed for a curveball but also made the ball drop. Most batters expected the flat curve ball from me and were surprised when they saw a dropping curve ball. It was an unusual pitch in my day, and it was my best pitch. I had complete confidence to throw it in any situation, especially in a 3–2 count. That pitch served me well, and I was sure old Tommy had seen nothing like it. He seemed relaxed, though, as he waited, leaning back on his heels and singing to himself.

"Just throw them in here, white boy."

I did and hit him on the inside of his right knee. The pitch knocked him off his feet, and he rolled around and hollered for a while.

"Hey, I'm sorry, but I warned you. My curves really drop, just like I told you."

He grunted at me as he got back in his stance. I threw him another curve, and it caught him on the left knee. Again he rolled around, holding both knees this time and yelling, "Damn, man!" He finally limped over to Mr. Sedberry. They returned after a few seconds of animated conversation, and Mr. Sedberry approached me.

"Mr. Craft, my catcher says you're hurting him," he said.

"Hell, yes, I'm hurting him. He's too old to play," I said. I stood with my hands on my hips, very sure that my opinion was correct.

"Mr. Craft, do you white boys like playing catcher?" Mr. Sedberry said while we watched the old man try to squat again.

"No, sir, we don't," I replied, taken aback by the racial implications of his question.

"That's right. It's a dirty, dangerous job. Do you think he likes it any better?" he asked, indicating the old catcher.

"No, sir. I hadn't thought of it that way, but I don't guess he would."

"That's right. It doesn't matter how old he is. Any time I can get a man to play catcher, I'm going to keep him around. He's a valuable commodity."

This was the first piece of baseball wisdom Mr. Sedberry imparted to me. I suddenly realized that old Tommy really wasn't that different from other white bullpen catchers who'd warmed me. They all strapped on heavy equipment and sweated in the dirt, and, as bullpen catchers, did this without the possibility of exciting plays at home plate or applause. We resumed our warm-ups.

A few pitches later, I let my fastball go. Old Tommy fell backward, but he hung on to it, and then smiled, gums shining in my direction. Mr. Sedberry saw him on the ground again. As the old catcher dusted himself off, Mr. Sedberry said to me, "You're warm enough. Go sit down in the dugout."

I had two pitches: a fastball that hummed and a sweet curve. I wondered if both pitches would challenge the Abilene Blues, some of whom looked far older than me. They had probably seen more years of baseball than I had of life. I had no illusions of turning the game into my profession. I didn't think I was good enough to play for a major-league team, but I was about to discover if I could hold my own in an all-black league.

The Abilene Blues took the field to begin their warm-ups in neat matching uniforms. They probably borrowed their name from a local white team that had stopped playing the year before, the Abilene Blue Sox. The Blue Sox traced their roots back to the Abilene Apaches of the West Texas–New Mexico League, which began play in 1939 but suspended operations during World War II. When the war ended in 1945, the league was reborn for the 1946 season as an affiliate of the Brooklyn Dodgers, and renamed the Blue Sox in honor of Brooklyn's trademark "Dodger Blue." They played in Blue Sox Stadium, but their connection to the Dodgers was short-lived, ending in 1948. The Blue Sox remained members of the West Texas–New Mexico League until 1955. When they moved to the Big State League in 1956, they began a two-year affiliation with the Kansas City Athletics, which ended after the 1957 season, the same year the Blue Sox disbanded.

At the start of the game, the Abilene Blues emerged from their dugout and taunted, "Are you even going to come out of your dugout?"

Sam pitched about as effectively as anyone expected him to, and the Blues scored seven runs in the top of the first inning. During the long half inning, our players took breaks to share a few drinks with the hometown fans. Everyone was feeling really good, except me.

The Stars didn't score in the bottom of the first, so the Blues were still far ahead, 7–0, in the top of the second inning. The Blues were having a great time, loading the bases with one out. I could see Mr. Sedberry's logic start working, but I was less than confident about my role in it. With the bases loaded, Mr. Sedberry called time and walked to the mound. He and Sam returned to the dugout. Sam gave me a grin, and then Mr. Sedberry slapped me on the shoulder.

"All right, Mr. Craft! It's time for you to go get 'em!" he said.

"Mr. Sedberry, it's too damn late," I said.

"Mr. Craft, trust me. I know what I'm doing," he assured me.

I strode reluctantly to the mound and started my warm-ups from the stretch. I just wanted to play my best and get my team out of the inning without any more runs scoring. Empty beer bottles started flying at me from the first- and third-base sides. I covered my head and backed away from the mound. The umpire called a timeout, and the infielders gathered the bottles and dumped them into the dirt behind the first row of seats in the stands.

During the timeout I walked over to first baseman Wayne Fisher and asked, "Why are they throwing beer bottles at me?"

Fisher smiled. "It's not because you're white. They do it to every pitcher, home or visitor. It's just a part of the game. It helps the fans pass the time and clear out the stands to make room for another couple of rounds," he said.

"I don't think this is such a good beginning for me," I said.

"Don't worry," he laughed. "They've had so much to drink they won't be able to hit you."

After the field was cleared of bottles and I'd thrown a couple of warm-up pitches, the umpire called, "Play ball!" I eyed the three runners and agreed to Alfred's signal, firing a fastball to the outside corner.

The batter hit a screaming line drive past my left ear. Fortunately, it headed directly toward second baseman Emmitt Johnson, who caught it and stepped on second for an unassisted double play. With one pitch, we were out of the inning. My new teammates celebrated, and Mr. Sedberry slapped me on the back as I returned to the dugout.

"See, it's starting to work, Mr. Craft," he said.

"Work? Did you see how hard that guy hit the ball?" I asked.

"Patience and faith, Mr. Craft," he said.

The Stars stranded two runners on base in the bottom half of the second inning. When I returned to the mound for the top half of the third inning, something was very wrong.

The batter, who was the shortstop and the coach's son, smiled at me. He was an average-sized baseball player, and he looked like a normal guy, but for some reason he wasn't standing in the batter's box. Instead, he was standing directly in the middle of home plate. I had never seen a batter do this, and I didn't know what to do next.

I called time to discuss the batter with my catcher.

"What's he doing?" I asked.

"Waiting for the first pitch," Alfred replied matter-of-factly.

"Well, let's try it again," I suggested, thinking that after the batter had a moment, he'd find the batter's box.

Alfred trotted back to home plate, and the batter again stood in the middle of it.

Again I called time. "I think we need Mr. Sedberry," I told Alfred.

I waved him over, and he began his methodical walk to the mound. The crowd was growing bored and again began throwing bottles, a few still full of beer, now warm from the West Texas heat.

"What's wrong?" Mr. Sedberry asked.

"What's wrong? Look at him! He won't stand in the batter's box!"

"Let's see what the umpire has to say."

The umpire, an enormous black man with a frown to match, moved around the batter, took off his mask, and asked us what the trouble was.

"Ump," I protested, "the batter can't stand on home plate."

"Why can't he, white boy?" the umpire asked.

"Because he has to stand in the batter's box," I said.

"What's that?" he asked.

"Well, you know!" I replied, but the umpire stared at me blankly. I was desperate for him to understand me and to acknowledge the rules of the game. "May I borrow your bat?" I asked the batter, who smiled and handed it to me.

As I drew the lines of a batter's box in the dirt next to home plate, everyone watched intently.

"There," I said. "The batter has to stand in there." I pointed the bat to the center of the box.

The umpire gazed at my batter's box, then up at me. "You mean, white boy, just because you drew those lines in the dirt that this man has to stand there?" he asked after I handed the bat back to the batter.

"Yes, sir," I said.

"Get your white ass back out to the mound and pitch before I throw you out of the game!" the umpire yelled as he resumed his position behind the plate. The batter returned to his position at the center of home plate.

I could hardly contain my disbelief. What was I supposed to do? I walked the batter on four straight pitches, protesting the entire time. The next batter was the left fielder and the coach's other son. He was a small, wiry guy who followed his brother's lead as he stood on home plate, displaying a smile both dazzling and mocking.

Frustrated, I called timeout again and motioned for Mr. Sedberry to advise me. When Mr. Sedberry finally reached the mound, more beer bottles started flying, along with some boos.

"Well, well, Mr. Craft. We have a problem," he said and laughed.

"Mr. Sedberry, I've never seen this happen anywhere before. Doesn't this umpire know what a batter's box is?" I asked.

"Of course he does, Mr. Craft. He's doing this because you're white. And I might add that he's enjoying it," he said.

"OK, what do you suggest I do?" I asked.

"It's very simple, Mr. Craft. Throw at his head," he said.

"What?"

"You heard me, hit him in the head."

"No, sir. I don't do that. It could kill the guy," I replied.

"If you don't, we'll lose this game. We might as well pack up and leave because all the batters will stand on home plate," he said.

I asked him if I could throw a brushback pitch instead.

"No, I think you should hit him," he said over his shoulder as he walked slowly to the dugout.

Alfred stood patiently, waiting for my reaction. I told my catcher, "I'm going to hit him in the shoulder or leg. Hard."

I assumed the stretch position and eyed the runner who had walked to first. I looked back at the batter, hoping that he had moved off home plate. He hadn't.

It was the scariest purpose pitch of my life. How would the Blues react? Would the batter's father kill me? Would the fans cover my broken body with beer bottles?

I gave the batter one last warning. He told me to shut up and pitch. Full of fear and adrenaline, I threw as hard as I could at his left shoulder. Instead of turning away from the ball, he turned into it, and it hit him right in the heart. Thump! He fell over backwards, his legs kicked a couple of times, and his eyes rolled back into his head.

"My God, I've killed this man," I whispered to myself.

I ran to home plate, and the batter's father sprinted toward him from the Blues' dugout. His son lay on the ground, quivering, and the Blues players poured water on him and fanned him with their caps until his eyes rolled back down. "Son, son, is you dead?" the coach asked.

"No, Daddy, but I almost is," he said.

"You white son of a bitch!" the coach yelled at me. He grabbed the bat and started to take a swing at me. I grabbed the ball and drew back to hit him between the eyes. He hesitated, but by that time our teams had restrained us. His boy finally stood up and staggered to first base, weaving back and forth over the foul line as he walked.

The crowd, enjoying the entertainment, chanted, "Kill him! Kill him! Kill him!" I felt like a foreign gladiator in the Coliseum, and I was sure the crowd wanted me dead.

The Stars' and Blues' dugouts were both empty, but no one really wanted to fight, and the teams slowly moved back to their original positions.

Over the next two years I never saw a single fistfight between black teams. They preferred to provoke their rivals verbally. Their vulgar language became a game within a game, each team discovering who could create the biggest insults. Players taunted each other so viciously that their words would have caused both benches to clear if they had been playing white teams, but the black players never intensely disliked one another. Regardless of who won or lost, the black teams wanted to visit with one another after the contest, and no one wanted to ruin the opportunity to socialize by fighting. The fans, on the other hand, would often fight in the stands, but I think that they sometimes simply had too much to drink and argued over things unrelated to the competition on the field.

As I returned to the mound, I thought to myself, "What in the world am I doing here?"

I turned toward the plate and glanced at the next batter. To my amazement, he was at least three feet from home plate, his eyes as big as saucers. His batting stance was completely rigid, with his arms stuck out straight in front of him as the bat shook in his grip. He was terrified.

Alfred grinned knowingly at me from behind his catcher's mask and signaled for a high, inside fastball. I threw slightly inside, and the batter fell to the ground. He resumed his stance far from the plate. My next pitch, a curve, broke for a strike. For the third strike, I threw a curve on the outside corner. Again, the batter hit the dirt. Alfred and I smiled at each other as I easily struck out three in a row. For the rest of the game, any time anyone got close to the plate, I threw under his chin, and he retreated. Then I'd throw curves.

The Blues' coach became increasingly frustrated, screaming at the next batter, "Be a man! Dig in there! What's wrong with you?"

"You come out here and bat!" the batter yelled back at him. The coach never said a word after that.

For the rest of the game, no one could even hit a ball foul. The Blues had lost all of their confidence. Even worse, they were afraid. Their offense and defense collapsed.

The Stars' confidence grew and matched the talent that they already had. They had simply needed a pitcher, and now they had one.

Amazingly, I struck out twenty-one Blues in a row, and the Stars defeated them for the first time by a score of 18–7!

As I struck out the final hapless batter, the fans, who had been drinking and celebrating for hours in the stands, moved their celebration onto the field. A large, happy crowd swirled around me, pouring out of the stands, running and screaming at me as I tried to leave the mound. I felt like Custer seeing all those Indians coming. I didn't know what to do, so I let them carry me off the mound. They paraded me around on their shoulders, fighting for the honor of giving me a cold beer. I had never played for fans like this before, and I loved it. I was hooked.

"Mr. Craft, you think you'll play another game for us?" Mr. Sedberry shouted above the noise of the laughing, celebrating crowd.

"Mr. Sedberry," I said, "I'm yours."

Two

Growing Up in Jacksboro

T HE STARS AND I CAME TOGETHER to play baseball for the
first time in Wichita Falls in 1959, but baseball and
racial segregation have a much longer history in our
area. In the late nineteenth and early twentieth cen-
turies, small towns in Texas like Wichita Falls and neighboring Jacksboro had their own white baseball teams, called
town teams. My father was a starting outfielder for a Jacksboro town team, simply known as the Jacksboro Town Team,
from 1929 until 1942, when so many men left for World War
II that baseball was suspended. The Jacksboro Town Team
started play again in 1946, but by then my father's ranch and
family kept him too busy for baseball. The team played at
Fort Richardson Field, which is now part of Fort Richardson
Historical State Park in Jacksboro. The park's eastern border

is Highway 281/199, Jacksboro Highway, connecting Fort Worth and Jacksboro.

Although no historical marker memorializes the baseball field, the shape of the lower part of the diamond can be distinguished at the north end of the park, near the munitions bunker. The bunker was built as part of Fort Richardson, which was in use from 1866 until 1878. The bunker walls stand about twenty feet north of home plate and are constructed from local stone, nearly three feet thick, causing the bunker's interior to be at least ten degrees cooler than the outside temperature. Small vertical slits in the stone allowed the soldiers from the Fourth, Sixth, Tenth, and Eleventh Units of the United States Calvary to fire their weapons from inside the bunker during skirmishes with the Kiowa and Comanche. The Fourth Calvary was led by Colonel Ranald Mackenzie and was considered the elite unit of the post.

When four companies of black troops from Kansas City arrived at Fort Richardson in July 1869, the white citizens of Jacksboro did not welcome them. Former Confederate soldiers were especially bitter and resentful of their new fellow troops. The locals thought the new arrivals were haughty, impudent drunkards, coming to town in large groups to drink and insult the populace. At that time thirteen saloons lined the south side of Jacksboro's courthouse square. On the soldiers' payday locals complained that they could walk from the square to Lost Creek, the northern border of Fort Richardson, and never touch the ground, stepping on passed-out soldiers the entire way.

The soldiers' racial tensions culminated in a shootout between a former rebel cavalryman, Joe Horner, and a group of black troops. When the troops demanded Horner buy them all a drink or suffer the consequences, Horner drew his six-shooter, killed two black soldiers, and wounded several more. The black troops retreated to Fort Richardson and reported the gunfight to their superiors. A white sergeant and six black soldiers arrived in town to arrest Horner, who had fled to another saloon. He resisted arrest, firing back at the group until they had to return to the fort. Horner followed on horseback, moving east and west along the banks of the creek. He aimed his Winchester rifle at a group of black troops who had heard about the incident and gathered along the other side of the creek to fire back at him.

Horner then killed a third black soldier before the horse he was riding was shot out from under him. When he ran out of ammunition, he strolled into Ed Eastburn's general store, the site of my present-day office building on Jacksboro's square, and purchased more bullets for his rifle and pistols while shots from the black troops filled the air. After slipping out the back of the store, Horner borrowed a horse and returned to his ranch north of Jacksboro. A few days later he decided to secure the services of an attorney. Together they met with the post commander from Fort Richardson and created a treaty. As I have heard the story, Horner "agreed not to kill any more Negroes if the Negroes would not kill any more of him," although Ida Laster Huckaby uses less colorful language to describe the event in *Ninety-Four Years in Jack County* (1949). Skirmishes such as these and battles with Indians raged until 1874, making the Texas soldiers and settlers too busy for playing baseball or taking steps toward racial integration.

In 1881, seven years after the last Indian battle, baseball began to emerge in Jacksboro and the surrounding areas, though the first teams were white. The two original town teams met at the Jack County Courthouse, both calling themselves the Western Pioneers. By August 1885, the *Rural Citizen* reported that a new Jacksboro team, the Red-Stockings, had organized a black-face minstrel show (Huckaby 1949). Although the reason for the show is unclear, the team may have been trying to raise money for baseball equipment. Two more Jacksboro town teams emerged in 1887, the Jack County Entertainment Independents (J.C.E.I.s) and the True Muffers. The *Rural Citizen* reported a box score for a September 29 showdown between the two teams, final score 37–25 in favor of the True Muffers. Jacksboro formed several other town teams from 1888 to the turn of the century, sporting the colorful names Featherlegs, Fat Boys, and Lean Men. Although their games lasted only an average of two and a half hours, they posted amazing scores of 47–44 and 26–20. Evidently defensive play improved by 1907 when Jacksboro star pitcher Roy Morton shut out the visiting Oklahoma City Indians (Huckaby 1949).

In those days, games between towns were highly organized social as well as athletic events. Entire families would travel by horse and buggy, later by car or pickup truck, for an all-day outing, including picnics and musical performances by the rival town bands at the Fort Richardson Parade Grounds, which included Fort Richardson Field. Railroad tracks for the Gulf, Texas & Western (also known as the GT&W or "Get a Ticket and Wait") line ran north of the baseball field. The elevated land that supported the tracks provided an excellent backstop for the playing field. Home plate faced south, and, as a bonus, Lost Creek flowed a hundred yards to the west. Fueled by Rumbling Springs, Lost Creek was the premier picnicking spot in Jack County, where hundreds of people would eat lunch and attend the games.

By the 1920s fans traveled to games in the several hundred automobiles that were rumbling through the county. Thanks to faster transportation, attending away games took much less time, especially if the roads were in good shape. They were two lanes of dirt that easily turned to mud after the slightest storm, and our Reos, Buicks, Model Ts and Model As, and Hyne Buggies were often not reliable. For that reason fans and teams generally limited their travel to a thirty-mile radius. When Jacksboro residents couldn't travel, Jack County's small towns, such as Antelope, Gibtown, Joplin, Vineyard, Wizard Wells, Cundiff, Barton Chapel, Jermyn, Post Oak, Newport, Truce, Perrin, and Bryson, played each other.

We owe a great deal of my family's history to the town teams and their games because they gave young people an opportunity to meet and socialize. The whole town closely monitored the events happening on and off the field. One of those fans, my Aunt Lois, was my mother's older sister. She married Ivan Oliver, Jacksboro High School's head football and baseball coach and superintendent. My mother, Louise "Lou" Johnson, was from Graham, Texas, thirty miles west of Jacksboro. In June of 1933 she met my father, Jay, during a baseball game at Fort Richardson Field, where she was sitting in the stands with Lois. My father had played ball for Coach Oliver in 1929, so the coach and his wife probably planned to introduce Lou to Jay at the game.

That day my father was playing left field for Jacksboro against the town team from nearby Antelope. Sometimes the Jacksboro team wore uniforms, but on this night my mother remembered that my father wore jeans, a white dress shirt, and a black bow tie. She thought that he was fast, handsome, and rather cocky. She also recalled what my Uncle Ivan repeatedly said about him during the game: "I coached Jay in high school. What a fine, single young man he is!" My mother sensed there would be an introduction following the game, and she anticipated meeting Jay. She kept a close eye on him while he played.

Trying to impress her, Jay stole home with his signature headfirst slide, and in doing so he ignited a box of matches in his shirt pocket. He was safe, but the crowd roared with laughter as the Antelope catcher used his mitt to beat out the flames. After the game, my Uncle Ivan waved Jay over to the stands.

"Jay, this is Louise. You can call her Lou," Ivan said.

"Ivan, would you allow me to take this lovely young lady for a ride in my Model T?" Jay asked.

"Yes, of course. If she wants to go," Ivan said.

My father said my mother hesitated for a moment, but he could tell she wanted to go with him. Finally, she agreed. Many years later she admitted to me and my sister that she was dying to go with him, but she wanted to play a little hard to get.

During their drive, Jay apologized several times for his burned shirt. "It looks terrible, and I'm sure it's ruined," he said.

"Don't worry. You have a clean undershirt," she assured him.

They were smitten with each other. After a short, happy courtship of three months, they were married, and my mother moved to Jacksboro.

My mother remained a fan of my father's athleticism well into the 1940s when she and I watched him play for the Jacksboro Town Team. Saturday night games were held under the lights. We had no concession stand, so we ate supper early before going to the game. Saturday night baseball was a family event, attended by everyone in the Jacksboro community. Even small children wanted to go, whether they had an interest in the game or not. It was the place to be. I can remember the cars lining all sides of the ballpark, including the outfield, because the field in Jacksboro had no fences. When the bleachers filled, fans set up chairs down the foul lines.

Dogs were welcome and frequently interrupted the game by sprinting across the field, seeking a player or owner. Kids followed the dogs as they marked their territory on the broom weed that grew near the field. Once the weeds were wet from the dogs' visits, the kids used barlow knives to cut the broom weed stalks and brush the damp weeds against the back of an unsuspecting person's overalls. The dogs immediately followed, this time marking the person as territory. The trick was a great crowd pleaser.

By the late 1940s, Jacksboro added lights to its field, the first in the area. From then on, crowds from all over the county watched night games at Fort Richardson Field. My family enjoyed those games because my father was slightly more relaxed when he played baseball than at any other time, but he was always the consummate competitor, encouraging his teammates to do their best. We admired his determination to win and his ability to concentrate on the game.

He extended his work ethic from the baseball field to our family life. When he returned to our home from the ranch in the late afternoons, he'd always hit fly balls to me and my younger sister, Linda. He hit baseballs to me and softballs to her. It didn't matter how tired he was. He would always grab a bat and drive us to excel. We were expected to become outfielders because he was one. We were severely admonished if we didn't dive for a ball and give the game all we could.

Over and over again we heard his motto: "When you work, work hard. When you play, play hard. Never give up!" He and his generation had survived the Great Depression. No matter what they accumulated in life, they never really felt secure.

My sister and I never completely understood my father's frugality, but we were glad we inherited his athleticism. He was a calf roper in his younger days, and we often went with him to rodeos. Later he traveled with the cutting horse circuit in the 1950s with his horse named Miss Texas, and they became the Reserve Champions of America in 1955.

Linda and I worked on our family's ranch and had our own horses for rodeos and parades. Linda was a natural athlete. Any sport was easy for her, which I resented. In high school basketball she would score twenty or thirty points a game, and I would only score eight or ten. I even gave up playing tennis because she would embarrass me in front of our friends. If I missed a tackle in football, the coach would call out, "Craft! It's a good thing they don't let girls play this game because your sister would beat you out of your spot on my team!" I'm almost certain the coaches would have allowed her to play baseball in high school if she had tried out for the team.

Linda and I played sandlot baseball together when we were children because there was no organized baseball of any type in Jacksboro until high school. We had no Little League, so our games were played on borrowed fields or in backyards. Nearly every day after school and on weekends after chores or church, we bicycled to Fort Richardson Field to play ball whenever the adults weren't playing. There were no set times. Kids of all ages just showed up and played, and we never knew who or how many kids would play, black or white. Sometimes we didn't have enough players for two full teams, but we didn't care because the games were strictly "pickup" games and we rotated through every position. I never had my heart set on one particular position because we rotated so often, though my father had trained me for the outfield. Our least favorite position was catcher because we had no catcher's mitt, mask, or pads. The catcher stood far behind the batter to avoid injury. For that reason, I didn't want to play catcher.

Fort Richardson Field was just south of Lost Creek, which bordered the black community in Jacksboro. Because the black children lived near the field and creek, they played and swam with us all summer. Baseball games always ended with a skinny dip in the creek's old Fort Hole. I thought it was bottomless. When I look at it today, I see it's maybe twenty by thirty feet and eight feet deep, but in my childhood it seemed as large as Lake Worth to our east. I remember that every child in Jacksboro, black and white, learned to swim in Lost Creek. Regardless of color, we played and swam together in the summers. I didn't consider how my friends from the Lost Creek community felt when they returned to their separate neighborhoods in the evenings after our swims. I was only a child, and it never occurred to me to ask them such a question.

Many of my childhood friends are still my friends. My best friend was Jim Boley, who now lives in Richardson, Texas. Bobby Murray, Tony Clark, Bob Sikes, Eddie McConnell, and I were also a close-knit group as children. We attended first grade together in 1943, and I knew they would be there when my mother dropped me off for my first day at the three-story red brick Jacksboro Elementary School building. At that time the school enrolled only white students, and on the first day of school I met a new friend, Leonard Jamison.

Leonard lived in the Cooper community, eight miles north of Jacksboro on Highway 148, near a land formation called Battle Hill, south of the Trinity River. His home stood near the hill, the site of a 1902 skirmish between Jacksboro's Sheriff Maddox and a gang of horse thieves. Alerted to their presence by a telegraph from the sheriff in Fort Worth, Sheriff Maddox quickly swore in a posse at Jacksboro and headed toward Battle Hill. Newly sworn-in Deputy Leftwich spotted the outlaws and the stolen horses near the peak of the hill. As I've heard the story told, he raised his pistol high over his head and shouted, "Follow me, boys!" He was immediately shot between the eyes, prompting the remainder of the posse to remember pressing chores at home.

Evidently, some Battle Hill bad luck had rubbed off on Leonard. He wore the unfortunate "country kid" uniform, coveralls. On the playground before school started, a huge kid named Bobby, who had flunked first grade three times and was the terror of the playground, started beating the daylights out of Leonard. I rushed over and tried to push Bobby off Leonard, but Bobby knocked me down and continued hitting him. Determined to save my new friend, I found a good-sized rock and aimed it between Bobby's eyes, knocking him out with a terrific pitch. His face had a very large bump for about a week.

The principal, Howard Elenburg, caught us both and gave me my first spanking. He then called my mother to take me home early. She was humiliated. Mr. Elenburg's paddling was nothing compared to my father's punishment for me. I had destroyed my family's good reputation before the bell had rung on my first day of school. My father told me I had to stand up to the bully the next day. I did, and, naturally, Bobby beat the dickens out of me, too. Every morning I dreaded going to school. Then I had an idea.

I arrived on the playground before school started. There I selected a few rocks and stuffed them into my right-hand pants pocket. When Bobby approached me and my buddies, I quickly pulled out a rock and drew back to throw at him. He slowed for a second but continued toward me. I threw one at his knee. The pitch was perfect. He winced and grabbed his knee while I took aim again. This time he scowled and walked away.

If I forgot my rocks, I paid the price. I'm sure the teachers wondered why I always had lumps in my jeans, but they never asked me to empty my pockets. Maybe the teachers were aware of my strategy for dealing with bullies.

Throwing rocks helped me survive elementary school and develop an accurate pitching arm. School bullies are great targets; however, it's one thing to avoid a fight and quite another to throw a strike on a 3–2 count. A full count is more stressful than a school bully because a full count forces the pitcher to stay in the game for at least one more ball or strike. I could always run from a bully, but I couldn't run from a full count. I would choose a bully any day!

Rocks soon became one of my favorite ways to practice baseball because Jack County had plenty of rocks. I threw them at tin cans when I was at home. Once during a sandlot game when I was ten years old, I threw a rock at a fast-moving jackrabbit crossing Fort Richardson Field and killed it. The kids talked about that feat for years, but I felt terrible. A couple of the poorer black children on our team asked me if they could take it home. Long, lean jackrabbits have tough meat compared to cottontail rabbits, so the rest of us would never have considered eating it. I felt better knowing that the jackrabbit would probably be in a stew that night.

Next I decided to work on my batting. I took a knife and whittled a flat board to fit a two-handed swing. My friends would pitch to me, and I practiced hitting rocks against our barn. A rock that cleared the barn was a home run. My father complained that the barn looked as if it had been hit by a hail storm.

I eventually developed a rather strange batting stance, lifting my left leg up and waiting usually until the last moment to swing, all arms and shoulders. I turned my head much more directly at the pitcher than other batters did because of the poor vision in my left eye. My unusual head turn worked for me, and I became a very reliable line-drive and singles hitter.

I remember that we continued to play sandlot baseball together on integrated teams when I was in elementary school because we needed at least nine players in the field. In a small town like Jacksboro, that was a large number of children to organize and agree upon one game. Whichever nine children were ready to play, black or white, we used them. The black kids didn't own gloves, so when one team was at bat, the other team used the gloves.

My white friends and I used old, flat gloves, handed down from fathers and big brothers, with one leather strip that served as the web between the thumb and forefinger. If the strip broke, and it often did, shoestrings were usually pressed into service as substitutes. Under such conditions, there were no one-handed catches. As soon as I caught a ball, I clamped my bare hand over it.

I remember receiving my first, honest-to-goodness, new baseball glove on Christmas Day when I was in fourth grade.

The glove became my most treasured gift that year. I used my father's Neatsfoot oil to keep it soft, the same oil he rubbed on his saddles. My new glove had leather strings connecting the fingers and a pocket, which greatly helped my ability to catch and hold a baseball. Compared to my ancient glove that had no pocket and one leather strip, the new glove was a tremendous improvement.

On the sandlot we all shared equipment, sparse as it was, especially the few bats we owned. We often used hand-me-down bats that had been tossed aside at the adults' baseball or softball games. As soon as we heard wood splitting or saw pieces of bat flying from home plate, we'd gather near the players' bench in hopes of receiving the bat's shattered remains. Cracked bats were highly prized because we couldn't afford new ones. We would nail the parts together and tape them heavily with black tape. They'd last a surprisingly long time.

Many of my sandlot baseball friends later played football and baseball in my front yard when my family moved to a large house on West Live Oak Street. At my new house, home runs cleared my folks' hedge of cedar trees. After games my mother would often bring us Kool-Aid. While we drank it, we talked about sports, hunting, fishing, and school, but I can't recall any of us, black or white, asking, "How come we have to go to separate schools?" We just assumed school had always been that way, and we couldn't conceive a world that would be different. After our snack, we played more football or baseball, and then we returned to our different communities in the evenings.

If the black children had opinions about living in a separate part of town or going to a separate school, they never mentioned them to me. Perhaps they understood at a certain level the inequalities of segregation, but at their age they could not verbalize their thoughts or didn't feel comfortable discussing them. In 1959 the city opened a segregated pool, which most of the white children used. After that, only the poor white children who could not afford the price of admission continued to swim at Fort Hole with the black children. I don't recall discussing the segregated pool with my friends either. I don't think we could have imagined the new pool, like Jacksboro schools, any differently.

Schools in my area had always been segregated. The first private school for white children opened in nearby Mesquiteville in the fall of 1857. The members of Fort Richardson Masonic Lodge then built the first public school for whites in Jacksboro in May 1870. The ground floor of the building was the school, and the second floor was the members' lodge.

In 1870 Jacksboro also constructed a beautiful three-story high school for the town's white students. Years later my grandfather, W. B. Craft, became the president of the Jacksboro School Board, and he handed my father his diploma when he graduated in 1929. My father, in turn, served as president of the school board in 1955 and handed me my diploma when I graduated that same year with fifty-five total members in my class. I always found that number easy to remember—fifty-five in 1955. About two hundred students attended the high school, approximately the same number enrolled there now. The school had about twenty teachers, coaches, and administrators, and the coaches, all men, taught both men's and women's athletics.

Finally, I awarded my oldest son, Jay, his high school diploma when I served as president of the school board in 1983. By the early 1980s, most of our town's school traditions had remained in place, except the building had changed because the original high school burned to the ground in 1962. A new circular high school opened in 1964, the same year the school system was integrated.

Before integration, Jacksboro had only one black school, the Blackshear Colored School, a one-room building that held both the elementary and high school. It was located on the banks of Lost Creek on land donated by a retired Fort Richardson serviceman. In the fall of 1888, sixteen students were enrolled in the school, whose total operating budget was $75.84 (Huckaby 1949). The amount budgeted per student was approximately the same as the amount budgeted per student for local white schools, between four and six dollars. When I started attending the white elementary school in Jacksboro, the Blackshear Colored School employed one teacher, Mrs. Linnie Shelton, who was from Jacksboro and had earned her master's degree from Prairie View College in 1918. As testament to her gifted instruction, a number of her students went to college and became doctors, lawyers, dentists, and teachers.

In those days, black people did not move easily from one town to another or from one job to another. Census records dating from 1919 to 1970 in the Jacksboro County Courthouse were arranged first by race of child and thereafter alphabetically. The census itself was titled "White Census Colored Census." Due to such divisions, we generally stayed where we were born, and we married and died there, too. In Jacksboro all of these activities were segregated, even burials. The northeast side of Oakwood Cemetery was reserved for the black community.

People my parents' age and older could not comprehend a world without segregation. For decades, state laws emphasized this division during elections. For example, a 1902 Texas law required that voters under the age of sixty pay a poll tax. Poll taxes had been collected in Jack County nearly every year from 1899 to 1945. Most black citizens couldn't pay the taxes and therefore couldn't vote. The poll tax was abolished in federal elections in 1964 by the Twenty-fourth Amendment to the United States Constitution and in 1966 in Texas elections by a state constitutional amendment.

The White Primary Law, enacted by the state of Texas in 1903, prevented black participation at the polls during the state's Democratic primaries. The law was eventually ruled unconstitutional in 1944 by the Supreme Court's *Smith v. Allwright* decision. Black and white people from my parents' and grandparents' generations had lived with official legislation that separated them and with the accepted division in races as the status quo for many years. I could understand why my older neighbors were very nervous about what they thought the Civil Rights Movement and integration would do to their individual lives.

While the senior citizens of Jacksboro, both black and white, did not accept change easily, some young, more progressive members of the white community recognized the injustice of this situation. In 1964 the Rev. Ed Gearheart from the local First Presbyterian Church and a group of young men, all of them white, asked the school board to meet with them so they could present their case in favor of integration. None of Jacksboro's black citizens appeared at the hearing. They cared for their community's school and didn't want to send their children to another school. They, like their white neighbors, feared change. Sending their children to the white school meant leaving their section of town, one that they rarely left unless they were going to work. For years they had lived under a large number of unwritten rules, including one that dictated they stay in their own section of town, where they were known and accepted. Their livelihood depended on following these rules. If they ventured beyond their neighborhood's borders without good reason, they were automatically suspect and unemployable by the white community.

Despite this tense atmosphere, the school board agreed with the group of white leaders that the school should be integrated. The Blackshear Colored School closed in the spring of 1964, and its only teacher, Mrs. Shelton, retired. That fall Glen King, a black freshman who was well regarded by the whole community, led his classmates from Blackshear into their new school. Glen soon became the captain of Jacksboro's football team and later was captain of the University of Oklahoma's football team. I've always been proud that Jacksboro's schools integrated peacefully, without the trauma that marred the process in larger cities. Perhaps our pleasant memories of summer sandlot baseball games and the friendships we formed there helped us integrate our classrooms successfully.

After the Jacksboro school system integrated, other formerly all-white areas of our town were soon opened to every citizen. The city pool was formally desegregated in the summer of 1965, but I can't remember any black children swimming there until several years later. I don't believe they felt comfortable swimming in the public pool with us, and they probably couldn't afford it. So, they and the poor white children continued to swim in Lost Creek.

When my friends and I started high school in 1951, our sandlot baseball games with the black children ended.

Instead, we all played sports at the white high school. We stayed out of trouble, but that was because no one caught us. However, I received the worst paddling of my high school career for a stunt I pulled during shop class. On that day I learned that I never again wanted to be on the receiving end of a beating with a baseball bat.

In those days we were required to take shop class. We built green cabinets or nightstands that were so ugly we couldn't give them away in a garage sale. I became terribly bored with the furniture project and started making key chains shaped like naked women from the leftover wood. I sold them for a dollar apiece. News got out about them, and soon I had a waiting list.

Of course I had to make them when our teacher, Mr. Price, was not in the shop. Before long I got careless, and he caught me. When Mr. Price found my offensive woodworking project, he announced to the class, "I have to go to town, and when I get back, I'm going to give old Craft the whipping of his life." I don't know if he really needed to run that errand of if he just wanted to increase my suspense and agony.

Mr. Price had graduated from Texas Tech, and he usually used his Sigma Chi fraternity paddle for his infamous two-handed whippings. As we nervously waited for his return, Jim Boley came up with a brilliant idea.

"Say, Craft, if I were you, I'd plane that paddle down to where it's paper thin. Then he can't whip you," he said.

What a heck of an idea! I planed down the side that didn't have the fraternity symbols. Everyone thought this was very clever, but then I had second thoughts and hid the paddle.

When Mr. Price returned, he asked me if I was ready for my whipping. I said, "Yes, sir," and he started searching for his paddle. He searched frantically, and I suddenly realized that harming an object so sacred to him was probably going to get me in worse trouble than sculpting naked ladies out of wood.

After he berated me about where I hid the paddle, with no results, he ordered the class to read our little-used textbook, pages one through twenty, in five minutes for a short quiz. Mr. Price composed the quiz from pages far beyond our reading pace, so we all made zeroes. He told us we'd have a quiz every day until his paddle was returned to him.

Several days later, he realized this tactic was not working, and he offered amnesty. If the paddle was on his desk in the morning, all zeroes would be removed from his grade book, and no one would be punished. Later that afternoon, I retrieved the paddle and placed it on his desk, confident all would be well.

The next day Mr. Price saw his beloved paddle, and a huge smile lit his face. Then he picked it up, noticed how unusually light and thin it was, and let out a half roar and half scream. He broke the paddle over his knee, and threw the pieces at the class.

"Get out your books!" he screamed at us, trembling.

With that, I stood up and told him I was responsible. He tried to get me to implicate others, but I wouldn't. I really wasn't being noble. Half the football team was in that class, and we risked our eligibility to play in Friday night's game if the zeroes continued. Mr. Price then went to Nash Hardware for a baseball bat. He planed it flat and gave me the worst whipping I ever had.

While I owe that pleasant memory to Jim Boley, I owe even more to my buddy Tony Clark, for he introduced me to the joy of reading. Tony played all sports, but he knew he could never be a great athlete because polio had withered his left arm. Despite this, he was a pretty good baseball player, and he and I were passionate about the sport, especially the Cleveland Indians, because at that time there were no major league teams in Texas. Our heroes were Al Rosen, Bob Feller, Larry Doby, and Bob Lemon. Tony was the sports editor for our high school newspaper, *The Tiger's Tale,* and for the yearbook, *The Fang.* He also covered baseball for the Jacksboro and Wichita Falls papers.

I always admired Tony's sportswriting. He created very colorful narratives of the action, many times embellished because he wrote about games in which he participated. Once during our senior year we played a baseball team from Iowa Park in Bi-District at Spudder Park in Wichita Falls. Tony played right field, and I tossed a three-hit shutout, final score 3–0. Tony's coverage of the game read, "In the fifth inning, Clark scored on Craft's sharp single to left field." I told Tony, "It was a broken bat blooper." He replied, "A hit's a hit, and this reads better!"

I didn't play baseball my first or second spring semesters in high school, 1952 and 1953, because our team didn't have a field. We were building a new field next to Lake Jacksboro, north of town. After spring football practice, the school would load all the high school athletes into buses and haul us to Lake Jacksboro where we used sledgehammers to break apart large layers of limestone at the site of the field. Tiger Field became a beautiful ballpark, overlooking Lake Jacksboro to the south with Highway 59 running along the first-base side. Even today a large purple wall of plywood sits on top of the outfield's chain-link fence to stop home runs. The dark color is also a good backdrop for hitters. Despite the purple wall, it is a hitter's park, with the left- and right-field foul poles a mere 250 feet from home plate and center field at only 300 feet.

My junior year, 1954, I won the starting job as left fielder, and Tiger Park officially opened. My father had trained me well. As an outfielder, I was tall, fast, and had a strong throwing arm. I could catch a fly ball and consistently throw the ball with one hop to our catcher. Of course, the short distance to the outfield helped. Most base runners in high school will attempt to tag up at third base, wait on base for the outfielder to catch the ball, and then run home before the outfielder can throw the ball to the catcher. I gained a reputation for throwing those runners out at the plate, and rival coaches soon stopped testing my arm.

We missed going to the playoffs when we lost our last game to the high school team from Graham, the Steers, because only the team that won the district championship advanced. I was voted a member of the first All-District team and had a batting average of .340, which was some consolation for not advancing to the playoffs.

At Jacksboro High School, our head baseball coach was Wallace "Hogcaller" Myers, so named by the *Fort Worth Star-Telegram* for his piercing screams. He took me aside at the end of the 1954 baseball season and told me that I had the strongest, most accurate arm on the team, so he would probably name me starting pitcher my senior year. I was excited but pensive. The pitcher, like the quarterback, was "The Man."

"Coach, I don't know how to pitch. I've never pitched in a high school game," I told him.

"Yes, that's a bit of a problem," he said. "We'll send you to Monte Stratton's Big State Baseball Camp in Meridian, Texas, this summer. Don't worry. You'll be ready next year."

Monte Stratton, an outstanding pitcher from Celeste, Texas, played baseball for the Chicago White Sox in the 1930s. He won thirty-six games in 1938, then accidentally shot himself in the leg while hunting. He tried playing with a prosthesis, winning eighteen games for Sherman in the East Texas League and seven games for Waco in the Big State League. However, opposing teams soon learned to bunt against him, and he couldn't move quickly enough to successfully field bunts. The situation must have left him in agony because while he still had a great arm, his opposition showed him no mercy. Jimmy Stewart played him in the 1949 movie *The Stratton Story*, costarring June Allyson.

Stratton's baseball camp was quite an experience for a country boy who had never been far from home. Tony Clark, my high school buddy, went with me as he was replacing me in left field. I was glad to have a friend from home along because the camp intimidated me. I had no experience with people from so many different places. Major-league hopefuls attended from Florida, Vermont, Oklahoma, Illinois, and, of course, Texas.

We were housed in an old three-story college dormitory filled with bunk beds and open windows. We could bring one small footlocker to hold all of our possessions. Mine was an old wooden army chest, painted black with my name stenciled on it. It held my favorite Nocona glove. I also had cut four holes in the chest, two in each end, to accommodate the two baseball bats we were each allowed to bring. I took my two favorite Yogi Berra thirty-three-ounce wooden bats with me.

High schools and colleges now use aluminum bats, which means players have highly inflated batting averages and large numbers of home runs. A ball hit with a metal bat travels at a much higher velocity than a ball hit with a wooden bat, creating impressive displays at the plate. While the offensive side of the high school and college game may be livelier due to aluminum bats, they also increase the chance that players in the field could be injured by a line drive or low foul ball. I often wonder what my batting averages would have been had I used aluminum bats.

While I was settling into Stratton's baseball camp, I noticed that one player had stenciled the name Jesus on his footlocker. I was stunned. I asked Tony, "Can you imagine anyone being bold enough to name a child after Christ?" His name, it turned out, was Jesus Salizar, and he was from South Texas.

The camp had excellent facilities and coaches. They divided us into teams, and we played and practiced constantly on four different fields. The coaches were from various colleges in Texas and rotated to a different team during each practice. Teams sometimes played games against each other, but we spent most of our days in separate practice groups: pitchers with catchers, outfielders together, and so forth.

The coaches knew what they were doing, and they were always offering me constructive criticism. I learned the value of controlled placement pitching. I had a strong, accurate arm, so the coaches really worked on my curve ball. They told me not to throw a flat curve. Instead, they asked me to snap my wrist down to make the ball drop, helping me to create my signature pitch, the dropping curve ball. This motion was very hard for batters to follow and hit.

I also learned the palm pitch, which is rarely used today. I gripped the baseball in my palm instead of with my fingers and threw it with the same motion as a fastball. The batter sees all the motion of the fastball, but the ball comes at him in slow motion. When used sparingly, it made a few of the batters I faced look foolish.

We didn't have sliders or screwballs back then, but the coaches showed me how to throw a knuckleball. I didn't trust it because when I threw it well, my catcher couldn't field it, and when I threw it poorly, the batter would hit it.

At baseball camp I also learned how to study batters, especially how and where they placed their stance. I started to edge over to the left side of the pitcher's rubber for left-handed batters. Throwing the ball close to their hands always jammed them up on the inside, making them unable to turn their wrists over when they tried to swing. They had a tough time against me. If a right-handed batter crowded the plate, I threw sidearm so that the ball would cross home plate at an angle. This strategy wouldn't work for lefties, who could see the same pitch better.

My camp win-loss record quickly climbed to 4–0. I might not have looked like a major leaguer in my blue Jacksboro Hull Chevrolet softball uniform, but I was beginning to feel like one. I knew I was making progress as a pitcher, even if I'd only been pitching for two weeks. I watched the other pitchers and thought they were much better than I was.

The highlight of each camp was the naming of the All-Star team, which meant playing a night game in Big State's stadium. I was delighted to be selected an All-Star, and Mr. Stratton, who was still coaching, named me starting pitcher.

"I know you're surprised," he told me. "But no one has worked harder or is more improved. You deserve a chance to start, and you've earned the right to do it."

I was stunned and flattered. I knew that if I wanted a chance at a college scholarship or a minor-league career, Mr. Stratton's school was the place to start.

For the All-Star Game, the Baylor University Bears of

nearby Waco came to Meridian on a Saturday night to play under Big State's lights. I was really nervous and wanted to do well. The Bears' leadoff man was ready. He watched a curve cross the plate for strike one. Next I threw close to his hands, jamming him on the fist with a fastball for strike two. He also missed the next pitch, a dropping curve, for a called third strike. I had struck out their first batter on three straight pitches.

I felt as though I was in control, but the opposition was not impressed. As the first batter returned to the dugout, one of his teammates shouted, "Damn, Fred, what's he got?"

Fred replied in an equally loud voice, "Absolutely nothing."

He was probably right. After only two weeks of training, should I have expected to beat a college team?

The next batter took my first pitch off the wall in right center for a triple. That was followed by a line drive that nearly took my head off, and after that pitch I was through for the night. I showered and joined the crowd in the stands, dejected, but my All-Star team rallied to win 7–6. At least I did not get the loss.

Before I left for home the next day, Mr. Stratton took me aside.

"You'll make an outstanding pitcher if you maintain your control, gain weight and strength, and develop confidence. Good luck!" he said.

I took his advice and worked hard that fall to become a better athlete by playing other sports, becoming a captain on our district championship football team and winning All-District and All-Area honors as center and defensive end. I also averaged eight points a game in basketball.

The spring of 1955 arrived. The grass was green, and baseball season began. I was in great shape from playing football and basketball. Our baseball team was soon a fine defensive club with fair hitting.

We played a standard seven-inning high school game. I became an aggressive base runner, ending the season with a total of twenty-two stolen bases. I was usually a line-drive hitter, but a north wind sometimes helped me hit home runs. At that time we never scouted our opposition in advance, had no game films to review, and there was no such thing as a designated hitter. High school baseball then was much more informal than today.

My fans in the stands were my high school friends. My sister and her friends attended the games, too. They all called me "Bubba" when they cheered. My mother and father rarely attended my high school games because games started at 4:00 p.m. on Tuesdays and Fridays, which cut into their work-days.

Although my parents couldn't be there, I thoroughly enjoyed playing high school baseball. The short distances to our home field's fences made me a better pitcher because I could not make any mental errors. If I left the ball up in the strike zone too often, a lucky child would run past the outfield fence to claim a souvenir. I believe I was born with a certain amount of pitching talent. I tried to develop my pitching speed by eating large meals, but I never gained the amount of weight I wanted.

I thought lifting weights might help, but my high school didn't have a weight room. Jim Boley and I made weights during our junior year by taking five-gallon buckets, filling them with cement, and sticking the ends of a metal pole in each bucket. They were ugly but functional, and they helped my pitching arm gain strength and endurance. I tried to develop other pitches, but to a certain extent, I already had my two pitches, a fastball and a curve ball, throwing them both as fast as I ever would.

I remember one high school game in particular against Bowie because it was the only time I became too sick to pitch during a game. Coach Myers and most of our players chewed Red Man Tobacco during our games. It was an admittedly bad habit, but many ballplayers at that time chewed. Bobby Murray finally persuaded me to try a bit of chaw before the national anthem.

The Jackrabbits' leadoff batter was a short, quick guy named Benny Carver. We had played football and basketball against each other, and we simply did not care for each other. During one football game against Bowie, I knocked him down twice in one play, and he was penalized fifteen yards for language. That animosity was carried into basketball season when a Bowie player hit the gym's brick wall so hard he passed out. The fans began throwing everything they could find on the court, and the game was called off. That night the Jacksboro team received a police escort from the gym to our bus, where we found its windows broken.

So, in a display of sportsmanship on my part, I quite naturally threw my best fastball at Benny Carver's head. He hit the dirt, got up, and glowered at me as the Bowie fans screamed for revenge. On the next pitch, he squared around to bunt, and I charged off the mound to field the ball if the bunt was successful. Instead of bunting, he took a half-swing, and I caught the ball in my glove against my forehead for the out. In the excitement, I swallowed the tobacco. After the next inning, I was as sick as a horse. Coach Myers, disgusted with the situation, replaced me with right-hander Johnny Geer, and we lost.

I redeemed myself against Bowie the following week at

home, Tiger Field. Without the help of tobacco, I threw a three-hitter and beat the Jackrabbits 3–1. Olney beat the Jackrabbits the following week, and we beat Decatur, so we won the district championship. I was especially happy that both my mother and my father attended the Decatur game.

I finished a very satisfying high school career with a batting average of .452, an 11–3 win-loss record, a 1.33 ERA, and only 1.33 walks a game. I hated walks. Nineteen fifty-five was a very good year in baseball for me. I was voted MVP of District 9—AA—but I knew that if I wanted to play regularly at the college level, I would need more experience.

After graduation, I stepped immediately into the semi-pro ranks so that I might have a better chance to play for the Texas Tech Red Raiders in Lubbock, where I had been accepted for the fall semester. Monroe, who was already playing at Tech, and I signed with the Jacksboro Roughnecks, who played on Saturday nights, and with the Midway Falcons, who played on Sunday afternoons. We enjoyed playing for them and hoped to be teammates in Lubbock, too. Earlier that spring, however, I thought I was on my way to athletic glory as a Texas A&M Aggie, but I soon learned that College Station was quite different from Jacksboro, where I had grown up loving my friends, my family, and baseball.

THREE
Experiences in Higher Education

N THE EARLY SPRING OF 1955, A. G. Beane, the principal at Jacksboro High School, started recruiting me to play football and baseball for his alma mater, Texas A&M University in College Station. Although I preferred baseball, football was, and still is, king in Texas, and the most talented college athletes primarily played football. In those days, full baseball scholarships were extremely rare. Student-athletes who played baseball often received half-baseball and half-football scholarships. The half-football portion of the scholarship always took priority, and the student played baseball only when spring football practice sessions weren't scheduled. If a walk-on football player showed more promise on the gridiron than the half-baseball scholarship player did, the other half of the baseball player's scholarship was promptly awarded to the walk-on football player. And, of course, football generated far more money than baseball, so universities often persuaded extremely talented athletes to give up baseball if they could play football.

Principal Beane saw my potential as a combination football and baseball player. He thought that the A&M football team could use me and my friends Bobby Murray and Jim Boley to improve the Aggies' record from their 1954 season, which was 1–9 overall and 0–6 in conference play. That year, 1954, was also the first year Paul "Bear" Bryant became head coach. He was confident he could help the Aggies recover from the staggering blow of their previous year's record. With that kind of season, I don't think a few athletes from Jacksboro could have possibly hurt them.

Principal Beane sent our football films to A&M, along with our high school football and baseball statistics. We were never visited by an official recruiter from A&M because scouting and recruiting in those days was very informal, especially for small schools like ours. The size of a school in Texas is designated by the number of As it is assigned. Our school was only a 2A school; the largest were 5As. In addition, my friends and I were not "blue chippers," the best rating high school recruits could receive. We had garnered some local and area honors, but we were not among the top prospects in the state.

Despite these factors, the A&M coaches liked what they saw in the films and offered both Bobby Murray and Jim Boley full football scholarships and me a half-football, half-baseball scholarship. We were thrilled because none of us had made any formal plans for higher education. Many of our friends were content to stay in Jacksboro and maintain their family's business, like cattle ranching. Through experiences like Monte Stratton's baseball camp, I had slowly become aware of possibilities in life other than working with cows in West Texas, and I became eager to leave Jacksboro.

To prepare us to become Aggies, A&M invited us to their traditional High School Athletes' Week in College Station. We excitedly packed our jeans and letter jackets and squeezed into Bobby's old black pickup on a Friday afternoon. Our usual companions on road trips, his family's hound dogs, stayed at home this time. They whined and howled as we turned out of Bobby's driveway and headed south to begin our six-hour trip to Aggieland.

Our parents had provided us many road maps, all highlighted, for the journey from Jacksboro to College Station. Interstate 35 would have been perfect for our trip, but it was still under construction in 1955 and had numerous detours. When completed, I-35 would be called the "Main Street of Texas" because it links four of Texas's largest cities: Dallas, Fort Worth, Austin, and San Antonio. Instead, we traveled two-lane highways, such as U.S. 281 and U.S. 6, through small Texas towns like Stephenville, Hico, Meridian, Waco, Marlin, Hearne, and finally into College Station.

Arriving late on Friday night, we were greeted by a few current students, including Jacksboro's own Paul Lillard, who was an All-State football player in 1953 and had become a guard at A&M. We were surprised to see Paul wearing a military uniform. He greeted us warmly and took us to a regular military dorm. High school athletes typically stayed in the military dorms while they were being recruited because the athletes at A&M were also members of the ROTC. In fact, we soon discovered that all the students wore military uniforms because everyone at A&M was in the military. We also noticed that A&M was still segregated.

Few universities in Texas had begun the integration

process in the 1950s. The University of Texas integrated in response to the 1950 U.S. Supreme Court decision *Sweatt v. Painter*, which required African American students be admitted to the UT School of Law, although they were not accepted as UT undergraduates until the fall of 1956 and not allowed into all dormitories until 1961. A&M would not fully integrate its campus until 1963. During our visit to A&M in the early spring of 1955, Jim Crow laws still ruled Texas, and the Civil Rights Movement had yet to gain true momentum in the southern states.

In this very military, segregated, male atmosphere, we were fêted and given tours of the Texas A&M campus. We were overwhelmed by the possibility of being Aggies, although we knew very little about the university. When the dorm residents asked us what branch of the ROTC we intended to join, we had no idea what an "ROTC" was. We were especially confused because the students pronounced it "ROT-see."

Bobby and Jim said, "No idea."

I really didn't know either, but I acted knowledgeable and said, "Armored Corps."

"Those iron coffins?" the members of the corps laughed. Suddenly my future athletic and military career at A&M did not seem so glorious.

The next morning bugles blared at dawn, and everyone scrambled to dress for breakfast. As we sleepily pulled on our jeans and T-shirts and staggered behind the rest of the cadets to the mess hall, three future Aggies started feeling distraught. We sat across the table from some freshmen, and they started eating at attention while upperclassmen constantly screamed at them. We could barely chew our food.

The day improved when we toured the football field and

training rooms. We had ushered at TCU football games in Fort Worth for several years as Boy Scouts, so we weren't awed by A&M's Kyle Field. We were soon enjoying A&M's spring football practices, dividing our time between them and watching A&M's baseball team play Rice. The baseball team looked good, having made their first NCAA regional appearance in 1951. They were to make their second NCAA regional playoff appearance later that spring, but we were more interested in the weight room. It amazed us.

We had never seen an official weight room, complete with exercise machines. We understood the concept behind lifting free weights, but we didn't know what the other machines were or how they worked. We were very impressed by them, but we were too embarrassed to act impressed. We had seen visitor locker rooms before high school football games at Weatherford, Mineral Wells, Dallas, and Diamond Hill, but I was always so nervous before games that I didn't notice any weight equipment, if they had any. By far the worst visitor locker rooms were in Olney, where football was played in the local rodeo arena because it had lights, stadium seating, and parking. The visitor locker rooms there had no urinals, just a lone toilet in the center of the room without any stall around it. Before one game the septic system backed up, so our pregame meeting moved outside. A&M's locker rooms were certainly a far cry from our football days, especially the rodeo's locker room with its lone throne.

After an interesting day watching football and baseball, we ate dinner in the athletes' cafeteria, where Coach Bryant addressed us. He welcomed us to A&M, touting its history and his plans to build the school's football program into a national powerhouse. He must have known what he was doing. In the fall A&M's record would improve to 7–2–1 overall and

4–1–1 in conference play. By the end of the 1956 season, A&M had reversed the 1954 numbers and posted records of 9–0–1 and 6–0–0. During his speech he never mentioned baseball. Why would he? His interest, like his school's and state's, was creating a winning football team.

Then he asked us if we had any questions. There was silence. Anyone with a modicum of sophistication or intelligence would never have dared to ask the feared head coach a question, particularly in public. So, of course, I raised my hand.

"Yes, son?"

"I have something that's been troubling me since I got here. Where do they keep the girl students?" Naturally, that brought the house down, but I was serious. My friends and I had wondered where the women were.

Coach Bryant stared at me, a look of disbelief on his face. His mouth hung open for a moment, and he finally asked, "My God, son, where are you from?"

After I told him, he said, "Son, there are no women at Texas A&M, and there never will be!"

Coach Bryant shook his head while laughter surrounded us. Bobby and Jim looked at the floor in shame. I didn't know if they'd want me to ride back with them to Jacksboro.

Our drive home the next day was unusually quiet. We even wished we'd had those damn dogs along to fill the extended silences of our trip. During that time we realized we'd probably never be Aggies. I was never happier to see West Texas than when we finally returned to Bobby's home, and I began thinking I would probably not go to College Station for school in the fall.

My faux pas with Coach Bryant may have also reduced A&M's interest in me. I never signed my scholarship commitment with them, and they never contacted me to find out why. The fact that there were no coeds at the school certainly shifted my plans in another direction.

Much to Principal Beane's disappointment, I applied to Texas Tech University in Lubbock late in the spring semester of my senior year. When I finally received my acceptance, all of the athletic scholarships were gone. Luckily, my friend Monroe Henderson, who had graduated from Jacksboro High School in 1953, was Tech's starting shortstop. Monroe thought the baseball coaches would let me walk on their team. He told me that if I was good enough, then they would probably give me a full baseball scholarship in the spring.

With the hope of playing baseball again, I began to look forward to starting school in Lubbock. There were many benefits to the university. At Tech I could be closer to home and enjoy the presence of the most beautiful creatures in the world, Texas women. I knew the Aggies suffered tremendously without them. Their loss meant we'd have more women at Tech, which made Lubbock even more attractive.

In addition to the social aspects of Tech, I liked the School of Animal Husbandry because I came from generations of ranchers. I was expected to get an education and return home to manage our ranch. My folks were pleased with my choice. My mother was especially grateful that I wasn't going to play college football. She had painfully endured each of my high school injuries, and she had no desire to see me hurt again.

During the fall of 1955, my first semester at Texas Tech, my thoughts slowly turned to becoming a more serious baseball player. At that time, the extremely competitive world of intercollegiate athletics was reserved for men. There were no women athletes because they had no scholarships. Instead, the coeds played a few sports at the intramural level in the physical education department. The philosophy was that women students who came to Tech for an education could benefit from being physically fit, but they were not tough enough to play college sports.

Tech, like A&M, placed a much greater emphasis on football than baseball, so most of my friends were football players. I lived in West Hall, Tech's dorm for athletes, because the university assumed I'd be a scholarship baseball player in the spring. While I enjoyed making friends with the scholarship athletes, I had to pay my own tuition, room, and board that fall, and the uncomfortable accommodations made me wonder about the expense. Three of us were crammed into a room designed for two, with two small closets, a twin bed, and bunk beds. I got the top bunk, but I had to lay my clothes on the floor.

My new friends, especially my roommates, Carroll Blessing from Fort Worth and Everett Putney from El Paso, took pity on my clothes and country ways and were determined to introduce me to life in the big city. I already knew a few upperclassmen on the football team, especially running backs Don Smidt and Jimmy Knox and center Bill Turnbow, because we had played football against each other in high school. My roommates and the upperclassmen took me under their wing, but it didn't take long for me to embarrass them.

One fall evening Don, Jimmy, Bill, and I left West Hall for a Friday night ritual at Tech, a beer run. We had to travel by car because Lubbock was dry; however, neighboring towns were not. Students could buy alcohol outside the Lubbock city limits, on the other side of certain alleys, and the locations of those alleys were among our first lessons at Tech.

That night I had the privilege of being the only freshman

on a road trip with upperclassmen athletes. They liked me because I was quiet and respectful, and they knew I was a good baseball player, which made me automatically popular. They had no idea I was very much in awe of them and their urban sophistication. We bought Jax beer, but I had never had a drink before. My first swallow gagged me. I had never tasted anything so vile in my life.

As my new friends were finishing their Jax, they tossed the empty cans out the car windows. Don became suspicious when I wasn't throwing anything away. I was in a real quandary because I didn't want my peers to discover that I had never been out drinking, but I couldn't swallow the foul brew. A solution dawned on me. I loudly announced, "This is great stuff," and threw a full can of beer out the window.

At that same moment we came to an abrupt stop at a red light. The heavy can hit the sidewalk with a resounding plop. The can then rolled merrily alongside our car, spewing beer along the pavement. Everyone turned to me in shock. I had committed a fatal desecration by discarding a full can of beer in a dry city. I had spilled our last drop of water into the desert, miles from the nearest oasis.

I felt deeply ashamed and turned ten shades of red as Bill asked me, "Why in the world did you do that?"

"I've never had a drink before, and that stuff tasted awful," I replied.

One of my roommates gallantly came to my defense. "Hey, leave him alone. He's just a country kid and doesn't know any better," Everett said.

Naturally, this led to the question that many kids from small towns like mine dread: "Well, Craft," Bob asked, "have you ever even slept with a girl?"

At that time, drinking and dating were essential to the identity of scholarship athletes at Texas Tech, and I was quickly losing my credibility.

I desperately wanted to lie, but I knew I was doomed. I quietly muttered, "No, sir."

"Poor bastard," Bill said. "Where are you from again?"

I was too embarrassed to respond, so I sat quietly.

"Are you queer?" Bob then asked, who was sitting next to me but scooting away.

"No," I said forcefully, feeling I had to defend myself. "I was always too busy with work, school, and sports for girls. I had a couple of girlfriends, but they weren't those kinds of girls. Jacksboro girls don't do that sort of thing."

A great sense of pity swept through our group. My new-found friends and benefactors quickly agreed to drive me to a certain house, and, against my wishes, saw that I was soon rid of my dreaded social status.

Like my new friends, most students at Tech were from West Texas or small towns, where college athletes were idolized. My friends and I were extremely popular on campus. During my first semester, Tech's quarterback, Jack Kirkpatrick, rode his horse into the Student Union, tied the reins to the back of a chair, and ordered coffee. He was told to leave his horse outside next time, but the administration took no further action against him.

This was not surprising because in the 1950s Tech was a sprawling country school, and its remote location caused us to be very tolerant of each other as we suffered the hardships of life in West Texas together. For example, the extreme weather in Lubbock, ranging from sandstorms to snowstorms, made playing college sports difficult. The unbearable heat and dryness of June, July, August, and September gave way to freezing temperatures in January and February. During the winter months a large complex of buildings on campus generated steam and piped it through nearly eight miles of underground tunnels to heat campus buildings.

My first winter at Tech passed slowly as I anticipated the start of baseball season. My football friends and I killed time by watching the antics of one enterprising upperclassman, a defensive back. He had discovered that the tunnels could supplement his scholarship money. He traversed them every night, making stops in certain buildings. He always had a schedule of upcoming tests and knew the locations of the professors' offices. He'd leave West Hall, and we'd all say, "Hey, look who's going to work!"

He wore old coveralls to protect himself from the vermin and filth that coated the tunnels. His miner's helmet lit his path through the darkness as he carried a huge ring of keys and his tool box. He entered a manhole near our building and would unerringly emerge in the basement of the Chemistry building or other planned destinations. He had keys to most offices. If the lock had been changed, he'd expertly pick and relock it, no one the wiser. His services were, understandably, very popular, and he drove the most expensive car on campus, a red Cadillac convertible.

In the early spring of 1956, when the pipes were still steaming, two ambitious athletes, a freshman tackle and a running back, decided that the defensive back had an unfair monopoly on such a lucrative business. The new entrepreneurs equipped themselves with protective clothing, helmets, and tools and began their maiden voyage to the English building. We watched them descend into the tunnels, shaking our heads because they had no idea where they were going. The defensive back had never created any maps. He had excellent spatial reasoning abilities and the good sense to know the danger of being caught with a map of the campus tunnels.

After wandering lost for some time, the freshmen decided to resurface to get their bearings. The tackle gently lifted the heavy manhole cover for a peek. They were close, underneath the parking lot of the journalism building. The tackle then noticed the wheels of a campus patrol car slowly rolling toward them. He tried to push the manhole cover closed, but the car ran over it, breaking eight of his fingers and knocking him on top of the player waiting below, who fell onto the steaming pipes and received severe burns on his back. The following day the campus newspaper, *The Daily Toreador*, reported the loss of two promising athletes to injuries suffered during a spring football practice. The paper said they would not play in the upcoming intrasquad scrimmages.

Baseball season finally arrived, and I felt like a real college athlete for the first time. I had played football and baseball in high school, but I didn't feel like I was a real athlete then because most of my friends were also playing sports. We all did it, so I didn't feel particularly special. At Tech, though, few students played sports for the university. Those of us who did were students first and athletes second, but I really loved being an athlete and a competitor.

After a few practices, the baseball coaches and players at Tech assured me that I was good enough to make the team and probably earn a starting position. I was excited at the possibility of being part of Tech's athletic department. The school had just been admitted to the famed Southwest Conference (SWC) and was finishing its last season with the Border Intercollegiate Athletic Conference (1931–61), whose original members were Arizona State, Arizona, Northern Arizona, and New Mexico A&M (now New Mexico State). Tech had joined the Border Conference in 1932, but when New Mexico left for the Skyline Conference in 1951, the Border Conference began falling apart. Northern Arizona departed after the 1952 season, followed by Tech in 1955. Tech's students did not mourn the loss of their membership in the ailing Border Conference. Instead, the announcement of their school becoming a part of the SWC caused the students to form a huge conga line and dance in the streets, temporarily stopping traffic and shutting down businesses. On May 12, 1956, *The Daily Toreador* ran the headline, "Extra! Finally! Tech Makes SWC, Tech Breaks SWC Jinx." At that time, the SWC also included University of Texas and Texas A&M.

During the spring semester of 1956, I continued my workouts with the baseball team as a walk-on member. Being a "walk-on" meant that the coaches had no scholarship to offer me and no guarantee that they could find a scholarship for me even if I played well and made the team. Our practices were informal, but I was encouraged when the coaches assigned a freshman catcher to me. Butch Ogden and I studied the varsity players, especially the pitchers, closely. They were more talented than the high school players we'd seen, but not overwhelmingly so. They were just older and bigger.

My workouts consisted entirely of pitching to Butch. Occasionally a coach would wander over and watch us. He would observe a few pitches, nod his head approvingly, and then move on. Butch and I could hardly wait to face some batters in a practice game. We wanted to know how I was going to fare in real combat.

I remember how excited I was when I received my Texas Tech uniform shortly before our first practice game. The jersey was light gray with black pinstripes and had "Raiders" across the chest in large, scarlet script. Our caps featured the famed double *T*.

For our first practice game, West Texas State came to Lubbock, and the coaches tried to give everyone a chance to play so that they could evaluate our potential. I patiently sat in the bullpen and waited for my turn. After a few hours, I finally heard a shout from the dugout.

"Craft, warm up!"

Our pitcher was in trouble in the top of the ninth inning. I thought I might get a chance to help him maintain our lead as I nervously started throwing to Butch. Unfortunately, the pitcher managed to finish the game without my assistance, and I never made it out of the bullpen. I had come so very close to pitching that I was eager for the next practice game and a chance to play. I thought to myself that at least they knew my name.

Following the game, we assembled in the Red Raider locker room for a team meeting. Coach Beattie Feathers stood to make announcements. He had been an outstanding college football player from Auburn University and was an assistant football coach for Texas Tech. Although he was also head baseball coach, I could tell that during practices he'd rather be somewhere else. He would often stare into the distance, watching the horizon. I sensed that he had no real affection for baseball.

"I've decided to cut some players who aren't quite college material," he said. "I've posted their names on the bulletin board in the hallway outside my office. Those on the list, please turn in your uniforms." He then retreated into his office, shutting the door on a room full of surprised ballplayers.

As we crowded around the list, I gasped when I saw my name. Of course there were other names, but that was little comfort to me. Monroe was as shocked as I was. He put his arm around my shoulders and said, "Let's have a really good summer in semi-pro, and then we'll try again next spring."

Monroe knew I was hurt. When I had a goal, I nearly always achieved it. This time the situation was completely out of my control. It didn't make sense. I had never been cut for any sport, and I didn't know how to handle the despair and rejection.

Monroe remembers when I was cut. He thought that I wasn't big enough and didn't look like a college baseball player yet. I didn't put on enough weight and muscle to look the part until I was a sophomore. I didn't understand that at the time, though. Instead, I was indignant about my rapid demise.

"I didn't even play in a single game! How could he have done this to me without even giving me a shot at playing?" I asked Monroe. Monroe had walked on to the Tech team during his first year in school. By the time he was a sophomore, he earned a full baseball scholarship. He was elected team captain during his junior and senior years. I thought that because Monroe had done so well, I would have a good chance to succeed, too. He and the other starters seemed a bit confused about my situation.

Players circled me, commenting, "We don't get it either."

"Most teams keep a young pitcher, even if he needs time to develop."

"Good pitching's hard to find."

"Don't give up."

I turned in my uniform, placing it on a large pile with the others, all representing players who were suffering the same deep sorrow. My dream of playing college baseball was gone, just like that highly coveted Red Raider uniform.

I wondered how the coaches could have missed my potential. On the surface, I was a tall, skinny kid who didn't throw that hard, but I was very sharp and knew the game. Given time, I would get bigger, but I guess Tech didn't want to wait on me. Years later Texas A&M's baseball program would pass on the opportunity to sign a young Nolan Ryan. Although Tech's cutting me isn't in the same category as that recruiting mistake, I would say that being cut from a college team doesn't necessarily mean the end of a baseball career. And that is just what I discovered once I joined the Stars.

A rude dismissal from Tech's baseball team gave me the opportunity to focus on academics during the remainder of the spring semester, which helped me more than I'd like to admit. In fact, I made the Dean's List.

I took my teammates' advice and during the summer of 1956 played for two semi-professional ball teams, the Jacksboro Roughnecks and the Midway Falcons. Monroe was the starting shortstop, and I was a starting pitcher. A few weeks into the season, a really good semi-pro team from Bowie noticed our play and recruited us, so we joined the Bowie team. The Bowie team had a better record than the Jacksboro and Midway teams did, and we liked winning, though we were really just happy to play baseball.

Bowie played teams in the Dry County League, named not for a lack of rainfall, though the land there often suffered from droughts. All the league's dry counties did not sell beer, wine, or liquor. We played teams from Nocona, Henrietta, Midway, Jacksboro, and Granbury.

Teams in the league picked up players wherever they could. One player would say, "I met a guy in the oil field the other day. He said he used to play semi-pro."

"What position?" we would ask. We were always looking for pitchers and catchers.

During one game at Bowie, we played the team from Midway. Monroe and I started the game. The Midway Falcons had a new third baseman who had played with Monroe at

Tech. When we removed our caps for the national anthem, the third baseman started teasing Monroe about his bald spot.

The comments worsened when the third baseman came to the plate: he called time, stepped out of the box, and told the umpire that he'd gone temporarily blind from the sun reflecting off Monroe's head. Monroe heard him and walked toward me on the mound.

"Hit this son of a bitch as hard as you can," he told me.

I hesitated, but Monroe added, "Do it for me."

I couldn't refuse my dear friend. As soon as the batter resumed his stance, I threw as hard as I could at his ribs. He fell to the ground from the force of the pitch, rolled over, and stood up. He then quickly charged the mound, bat in hand. Monroe intercepted him, glad to have the chance to fight until his team restrained him. I never saw Monroe lose his cool again. As we rode home together that afternoon, he told me, "I owe you one."

Monroe remembers another game I was pitching. We had a set of signals to pick runners off second base when Monroe was playing shortstop. Monroe gave the signal, and I turned to throw to him. The runner returned to second safely. Monroe gave the same signal again, and I threw, but the runner was safe once more. Monroe gave the signal a third time. I turned and threw the ball into center field. It was a beautiful throw. The fans and players stared at me as the startled left fielder chased the ball and the runner on second headed home. Monroe didn't say a word to me on the field. He acted like the run was my fault because I threw the ball. I was mad, but he was laughing.

After the game he told me, "Craft, I screwed up." I was a little angry at him. I had a hot temper on the field because I was competitive. Monroe was competitive, too, but he didn't want to take the blame on the field for not covering second base.

By the end of the summer of 1956, I was a seasoned semi-pro baseball veteran, two inches taller and thirty pounds heavier, measuring 6'2" and 185 pounds. I could move quickly, and my fastballs were hopping.

Yes, I had matured physically, but mentally was another story. We returned to Tech in the fall, and I moved to Doak Hall because I was not an athlete and didn't plan on being one. Tech's coaches visited me in the fall of 1956 and the winter that followed, encouraging me to walk on the baseball team again in the spring. I refused their offer. I felt indignant that I had been cut the year before, and my pride prevented me from accepting the opportunity to try again, which I now deeply regret.

Decades later I can admit that my wounded ego got the best of me, and I also disappointed Monroe, who wanted me to try out again. I would not even go watch him play. Instead, I played intramural softball in the spring of 1957 and was named the All-College third baseman. Monroe continued to play varsity shortstop for the Red Raiders, was named team captain, and graduated Tech in May 1957.

After Monroe completed a solid college baseball career, he and I played in the Oil Belt League for the Cruise Tire Company in Wichita Falls for the summers of 1957 and 1958. We never talked about our missing a chance to play together at Tech. He didn't want to make me feel worse about the situation. Instead, we enjoyed our new league, which included local baseball teams that were sponsored by area businesses. We played most of our games at Spudder Park.

During the summer of 1957, Monroe had his chance to repay me for hitting that Falcon third baseman. My sister,

Linda, and a few of her friends from Jacksboro came to see us play. They started yelling at a group of four guys who were rooting for the other team. I didn't like what the group was yelling back at my sister, but I was pitching, so I couldn't do anything to defend her until after the game. I mentioned my plans to Monroe between innings.

"No, I don't think you want to fight them," Monroe told me.

"Did you hear what they called my sister?" I asked him. He nodded and knew he couldn't prevent the fight.

Monroe remembers Linda was tough and probably a better baseball player than I was. She wasn't afraid of yelling at everybody she saw during a baseball game.

As soon as the game was over, I vaulted over the dugout and ran to the front entrance of the stadium. From there I could see one of the guys in the portal shouting at my sister, who was above him in the stands.

I ran up behind him and pushed him in the back, yelling, "I'm going to whip your ass!"

"Get him, Bubba!" Linda yelled.

The other three guys appeared next to him. "You think you can take all of us?" one of them asked.

"Oh, I think he's got all the help he needs." I turned to see Monroe behind me, holding a baseball bat.

I continued defending my sister's honor, calling those guys every name in the book, until they left the ballpark. They wouldn't fight once they saw Monroe and his bat.

"We're even," Monroe told me.

The visitors decided it wasn't over, though. They called the league's president and reported my behavior. The president requested I meet him in his office at the City National Bank Building.

"You're supposed to provide entertainment for the

citizens of Wichita Falls, not threaten to beat them to death with baseball bats!" he told me. "I'm fining you $50."

"I was defending my sister. It was worth it," I replied.

Despite our undeserved reputation as troublemakers, Monroe and I returned to the Oil Belt League for the summer of 1958. The league gave us blue jackets with a white and blue baseball emblem on the front that read, "Oil Belt League, Semi-Pro, 1958." I still have the emblem, moth-eaten and framed, hung in my office.

That summer our Cruise Tire Company team tried the old hidden-ball trick. Those kinds of trick plays have been abandoned for years and years, but we still tried them occasionally back then. I gave a signal to our first baseman. Then I walked over, stuck the ball in his glove, and walked back to the rubber, acting like I had the ball. I couldn't actually step on the mound because the umpire would call a balk, but I could get close to the mound, close enough. The runner, believing I had the ball with me, took his lead off first base. The first baseman then tagged him out with the ball. The play was perfectly legal, but major-league players didn't try it. They knew better. Our small-town leagues, however, were perfect for it. When our team was at bat, we would always make sure that the opposing pitcher didn't hand the ball to the first baseman when we had a runner on first. It was a funny little trick.

The highlight of that season with the Cruise Tire Company team was a two-hit shutout I pitched against an old rival, Harvey Klinkerman. He had pitched for Texas Tech, so I was eager to prove that I could compete against him. We played at Iowa Park, and I struck out thirteen batters that game, defeating Klinkerman easily.

The summer passed quickly, and during the season's last

game, Monroe and I were named league All-Stars. If that wasn't enough glory, the Cruise Tire Company awarded us each a set of tires for our fine performances.

As we were presented our tire coupons, a stranger approached us. He wore a straw hat and a neatly pressed white cotton dress shirt. He introduced himself as a scout from the Boston Red Sox and gave me his business card.

"Heck of a game, Mr. Craft. Have you ever considered a career in professional baseball?" he asked me.

"No, sir," I said. The thought had never crossed my mind, especially after I was cut from Tech's team.

"Why?" he asked.

"I don't think I'm good enough," I said.

"You most certainly are," he said. "Here is our standard contract. It doesn't have your name on it, but it shows you what your salary would be. You study that and call me if you have any questions. I think you could play for the Red Sox."

I thanked him, and I couldn't think of anything else during the long drive back to Jacksboro. I rode with Monroe, and we talked about my major-league prospects. Monroe had already tried out for the Baltimore Orioles. He proudly wore their uniform in the Oil Belt League. The Orioles had even offered him a contract, but Monroe declined so that he could finish his classes and graduate from Tech.

Monroe had also tried out for the Washington Senators, who had a farm club in Midland. He remembers that he spent a few days there, and he really wanted to play for them. He kept thinking, "Am I good enough to do this?"

When Monroe left his tryout in Midland, he told the team, "You call me, or I'll call you." He didn't hear from them, so he decided to forget about playing baseball professionally. Instead, he focused on courting his steady girlfriend. When he finally got a good offer to play professional baseball, he was already engaged. Albuquerque called him the morning after he proposed and offered him a Double A contract.

"I can't do it," Monroe said.

"Why?" the caller asked.

"I've got other commitments," Monroe said.

I asked Monroe how he asked his wife to marry him, but he doesn't remember that evening. I think it's funny that Monroe can't remember the proposal, but he remembers the call from Albuquerque.

He believes if he hadn't gotten engaged the night before he might have signed the contract, but that morning he couldn't do it. He had already decided that he wasn't that good. We both enjoyed kicking around the little local leagues, but I don't know if we could have played professional baseball.

Monroe had told me after his tryout, "If you're really good, then you have to go for it. If you're not, then it's not a good life. I don't believe I was really good enough." The farm teams would be traveling in old, beat-up buses. Trying to make a living and supporting a wife while playing baseball at that level would have been tough.

Because he already had a contract offer, I listened carefully to him as we discussed my opportunity. Bear in mind that professional baseball was quite different in the late 1950s. A tremendous number of teams existed, ranging from Class D or "Rookie League" through Class C, Class B, and then Single A, Double A, Triple A, and up to the major leagues, all paying virtually nothing. Although there were fewer major-league teams than today, the large number of minor-league teams meant scouts were everywhere. They looked for talent, paid little for it, and stocked the affiliated minor-league teams with more players than would ever play in the major leagues. Monroe and I, no doubt, would have spent our first year playing on a Class D baseball team, and we had no guarantee that we would be on the same team.

"I already made my decision. Now, what are you going to do?" Monroe asked me.

"I really don't know what to do," I said. The West Texas countryside rolled by as Monroe tried to help me decide what I wanted to do with my life.

We both loved the game, and here was my chance, but how much of a chance did I really have? Because I had played against a number of former Double A and Triple A ballplayers during our semi-pro days, I knew I was talented but not exceptional. Monroe then made a great suggestion.

"Hey, let's analyze each other's strengths and weaknesses," he said.

"I don't think that would be good for our friendship," I said.

"It will be OK," he said. "Let me tell you what I think about you first. You've got great control and confidence on the mound. You may be the smartest pitcher I know because you study hitters so well and you use your head quite a bit. You're a good pitcher because you don't try to blow it by the batters all the time, but you can when you really want to. You have a good changeup, and you've got the best dropping curve ball I've ever seen," he said.

"Good," I said. "Now tell me the bad news."

"Your fastball," he said. "It's just not fast enough."

"Yes, I know. How far do you think I could go anyway?"

"Maybe Double or Triple A, and I'm not sure how successful you'd be there," he said. "Now, do your worst. Tell me about me."

"You are a great fielder. You are graceful and have a

cannon for an arm. And, of course, you can hit, but you can't run, not fast enough to steal bases on a good catcher," I said. "I think you can play Triple A ball."

We sat in silence for several miles, not unhappy with one another, but deep in thought about our futures.

"Monroe," I finally said. "I can't see myself riding around in a broken-down old bus for five years, playing in small towns."

He smiled and said, "Let's get on with our lives. I'm happy I decided not to play minor-league baseball. I'm sure you'll eventually find a nice girl to marry, and then we'll have kids and ranches. Until then, we could continue playing semi-pro baseball during the summers."

"Yeah, a set of new tires isn't such a bad deal," I said.

While we were pleased that a scout had noticed me, we were confident that we had made the right decisions for our lives. We knew we would be friends for a long time.

What I could never have predicted was that another scout, a player from an all-black team, had also seen me pitch during the summer of 1958. I had no idea that my baseball career would be extended with the Stars. If I had signed the Red Sox contract, I might have missed the opportunity to play for Mr. Sedberry and his team.

Four
Becoming a Star

R. SEDBERRY AND HIS CATCHER, Alfred Ray, had spent several Sundays in 1958 scouting me as a pitcher for their ball club. Both scouts from the Stars came to the conclusion that I was the pitcher they wanted for the Stars. The problem? How were they going to convince a local white boy to play in an all-black league in a highly segregated part of Texas during the beginning of the Civil Rights Movement? They solved that problem by omitting the fact that they were black when they contacted me at the beginning of the summer of 1959, perhaps hoping my love for the game would solve any challenges my being white and their being black would create. After that first game, they knew they had found the perfect pitcher, and I had found a great team, but we faced many difficulties during our first season together, a season that ended in tragedy.

During the summer of 1959, the first of my two summers

with the Wichita Falls Stars, my black teammates began the long process of accepting me. In retrospect, the process of my becoming a team member was twofold. First, my black teammates rapidly grew to know me as an athlete and as a winner, the dominating pitcher they had looked for to complete their team. Second, they slowly accepted me as a person, an equal though minority member of the West Texas Colored League community.

In my first game as a Star, I had helped them defeat their old nemesis the Abilene Blues in Wichita Falls. Afterward, the Blues created several excuses for not playing us again, but they finally agreed to a game in Abilene. On July 18, 1959, in front of a large crowd, I struck out fourteen batters. The Blues seemed intimidated when they faced me for the second time. I threw a close, brushback pitch to their leadoff batter to reestablish my dominance. Then I used the brushback pitch fairly often on other batters, followed by curves. I could feel the difference in the Blues' attitude. They had lost confidence in themselves, which happens sometimes.

I knew that feeling, too, when I would come to the plate against certain pitchers. It didn't particularly matter what they threw. The pitch would be delivered with such confidence and command of the strike zone that I didn't stand a chance. Luckily, the Blues' pitcher lacked control that day, and we won 6–0, my only semi-professional no-hitter. I still have the game ball, bearing the event, date, and score: "No-Hitter, July 18, 1959, W. F. 6, Abilene Blues 0."

The Stars were winners with me. Yes, I was white, but I was the pitcher the Stars had been lacking. Further, no matter my color, I knew how to compete and win. After games, Rabbit always said to me, "When you show up, we just feel like we are unbeatable. We're proud to have you. You're a friend of mine. We're teammates, and I'm on your side, regardless."

Segregation had little effect on Rabbit. It didn't seem to bother him quite as much as it did the other players. Rabbit understood we still lived in separate communities, but he made friends with everyone, including me. Years later Rabbit told me how much the Stars wanted me to play with them and how much everyone enjoyed having me on the team. They all asked Mr. Sedberry to give me a call before games. Mr. Sedberry knew I didn't need the reminders because I was very organized, but he called me anyway. I think they were letting him know they were happy with my pitching. They liked me so much that they did not care what the opposing teams thought of me. Rabbit once said about those years, "After we got to know you, we were on your side. We stuck with you."

Once the Stars began acting graciously toward me, I wished I had been more comfortable sharing news about them with my own community, including my family. At first not many white people in Jacksboro knew about my playing baseball with an all-black team. I didn't tell my neighbors, but I certainly wasn't embarrassed about the Stars or I wouldn't have stayed with them for two years. I simply omitted news about the team from my conversations with the families in my neighborhood. We lived in a small town, and I knew they would discover what I was doing on their own.

I've also been asked about my parents' reactions to the Stars. After I played my first game with them, my father asked me, "Well, how was your game? Did you win? What was this new team like?"

"Well, hey, I got some news for you. They're a black baseball team, and they play in a black baseball league," I said.

"Surely you're not going to play with them again," he said.

"Yeah, I am. I enjoyed the game, and they have a really talented team," I said.

"I don't want you doing this. It's an embarrassment to our family for you to be seen with a black baseball team," he argued.

"Well, I'm going to do it," I said, stubborn as always.

"I don't guess I can stop you. For God's sake, don't tell anybody," he relented.

I remember part of my separating myself from my father and growing closer to the Stars included throwing my new teammates batting practice. We didn't have many pitchers, so everyone, ace or reliever, pitched batting practice. I really enjoyed throwing batting practice for Rabbit. He wasn't a very big man, but he stood at the plate like he owned it. I would frustrate him because he couldn't hit my curve ball. Sometimes his easygoing smile would fade as he waited for his pitch, a high fastball. If I let a fastball get chest-high on him, it was gone. His smile returned as he watched the ball clear the fence. Batting practice was the only time we ever faced each other as pitcher and batter, so we really enjoyed it. I watched him hit many opposing pitchers' curve balls and fastballs out of the park, but he could never hit my curve.

Because the Stars and I could play baseball well together, we quickly started treating each other as teammates. We played the same game, by the same rules, and we loved it. I looked forward to seeing them and to playing our games. I could see from their reactions to me when I arrived at our games that they were really happy to see me. They would smile and wave as I approached the field. My presence gave them hope and encouraged them to play better baseball. When a team has hope, playing together is a lot more fun.

Although we had baseball in common, our personal lives were very different. I didn't know them, and they didn't know me, other than the fact that I was a different color. Our starting catcher, Alfred Ray, had grown up in my hometown, but we didn't know each other except as children on the sandlot baseball fields. After we started high school, our lives became more segregated, and we didn't see each other around town. We didn't stop on the street to discuss the local news or eat in the same restaurants. I knew Alfred's world existed, but it never touched mine.

Because we lived in such separate worlds, the Stars' and my shared passion for baseball had limits. We could discuss at length the technical aspects of the game, such as the strengths and weaknesses of the pitcher for the Grandfield Zebras, but my teammates had no interest in who was playing for the New York Yankees. The Stars did not seem to care one whit about major-league baseball players, black or white. Major League Baseball was another world to them, one that still lacked significant diversity. My teammates also disliked the way white players and fans in the majors could be hostile toward black players. Bear in mind that the majority of my teammates were from humble means and small, segregated towns with limited access to large cities. Instead of talking about the majors, Mr. Sedberry and Bobby Lee Herron discussed the Negro Leagues and their great old-timers. I would pay attention to their discussions, but none of my other teammates showed any inclination to broaden their knowledge of baseball beyond their Sunday afternoon and Wednesday night games with the Stars.

Similarly, I had little knowledge of the now legendary giants of the Negro Leagues. Mr. Sedberry knew all the players' names, but I didn't recognize them. With the integration of Major League Baseball more than a decade old, Mr. Sedberry recognized the inevitable demise of his black baseball universe. He knew that the Negro Leagues and our small West Texas Colored League would soon fade permanently. The formerly all-white major leagues actively recruited black players, and the Stars' steady fan base would leave us to listen to games on the radio or to watch them on television. Our little league was holding its ground, but not for long.

When I think back to 1959 and the transitions taking place in my country, in my life, and in the lives of those around me, I realize that I spent my first season with the Stars simply getting to know them. I'm still a little surprised they took the time to get to know me. I, quite frankly, didn't have any idea how they lived, and they knew nothing about me other than what they saw on the baseball field shortly before and after each game. We never had any reason or opportunity to inquire about our personal lives. Essentially, we lived in two different worlds and accepted them because we'd never known any other way to coexist. We were slow to ask one another personal questions. However, human curiosity eventually made them want to know me better as a person. I'm sure they often wondered to themselves, "What in the world would make a white person want to play with a black team?"

Few white people knew the answer, and even fewer had the chance to play with a black baseball team. One big exception was Eddie "Lefty" Klep, a white pitcher from Erie, Pennsylvania. He signed a contract with the Negro Leagues' Cleveland Buckeyes in March 1946. The Buckeyes had faced Klep and the Glenwood All-Stars, a team of local white players, on September 11, 1945, during a benefit game designed to help the Buckeyes prepare to face Pennsylvania's Homestead Grays in the Negro League World Series. The Buckeyes and their owner, Ernest P. Wright, Sr., liked Klep, and after Wright's team beat the Grays to become the world champions, they offered Klep a contract and invited him to spring training. Klep's experiences with the Buckeyes are chronicled in Larry Gerlach's article "Baseball's Other 'Great Experiment': Eddie Klep and the Integration of the Negro Leagues." According to Gerlach, Klep signed with the Buckeyes because he loved baseball and wanted more than anything to become a professional ballplayer.

During spring training, Klep was prevented several times from realizing his dream. He could not play his first scheduled game in Jacksonville, Florida, because a local ordinance prohibited the racially mixed team from using the city's facilities. A second attempt in Birmingham, Alabama, resulted in police officers demanding that unless Klep remove his uniform and wear street clothes while sitting in the white section of the stands, the game would not be played. Klep and the team complied with the wishes of Alabama's law enforcement officials. Frustrated, the Buckeyes' management returned Klep to the North so that he could train until the team arrived in Cleveland in April. Wright would not tolerate such treatment of his player and traveled back to Cleveland with him.

On April 7, 1946, in Atlanta, Georgia, Klep finally got his chance to play with a black baseball team when he and the

Grays faced the Atlanta Black Crackers. He pitched the first three innings and got the win, 4–2. Due to racial tensions, he never pitched in the South again. When the team returned to the North, Klep pitched in relief on May 29 in Grand Rapids, Michigan, against the American Giants. He earned his first regular-season Negro League win, 8–6. Klep's final appearance with the Buckeyes was on June 2 in Cleveland against the Indianapolis Clowns. He entered the tied game in the ninth inning, but the Buckeyes lost, 11–8. The Buckeyes released him shortly thereafter, claiming that he was not good enough for the league.

Klep pitched a total of three games for the Buckeyes in 1946, the same year Jackie Robinson first played organized baseball for the Montreal Royals, a farm team for Branch Rickey's Brooklyn Dodgers. My debut with the Stars happened thirteen years later, which I think was good timing. As Klep had been prevented from playing baseball in Jacksonville and Birmingham, I could have been prevented from playing in West Texas if any white city officials or law enforcement officers had been aware of my presence at the games, though the West Texas Colored League had none of the media exposure that the Negro Leagues did. Another difference between my and Klep's experiences was that my teammates were also probably much more ready to accept me than Klep's were, though the Stars and I needed at least two seasons to get to know each other.

For the first half of our first season together, my teammates were happy to play baseball with me, but we seldom conversed about anything besides the sport. After the first several games, however, they slowly learned to trust me with other topics, perhaps because our time together coincided with the troubled beginning of the Civil Rights Movement. Their first probes into my personal life came during tailgating parties, the small social gatherings that occurred after games as we relaxed, surrounded by their families and friends.

We would sit under trees to escape the Texas heat, or we would fold down the tailgate of a pickup truck, sit on it, and dangle our feet over the side. They would chat about everyday events, and I would listen attentively. I liked them, and I guess getting to know someone from another race during that time only happened if you liked them. Baseball gave me the unique opportunity to like them as teammates and then as people. Interacting with them was the only way I could get to know them. There were no news stories or books about the black people in my town. I was one of the few white people who spoke to them regularly.

In a June 1998 interview for the *Dallas Morning News*, Bryan Woolley referred to me as "Jackie Robinson in reverse," but during those days I never pictured myself like that. I was only ten years old when Jackie started playing for the Brooklyn Dodgers. I can't recall seeing him play for the Dodgers in 1947, the year he broke the color barrier; my family did not own a television set until 1950. If I had seen him play during his first season, maybe I would have thought of myself as a Jackie Robinson in reverse. Perhaps I would have emulated Robinson's quiet dignity.

During the 1950 season, I watched Robinson and read about him in the newspaper. He was a natural athlete and had intelligence, bearing, and good looks. His way of silencing his enemies was to keep his mouth shut and remain poised, exhibiting immense self-control under the toughest conditions. He let his playing skills speak volumes. I could have learned much from his experience and style. Instead, I had to do it my way.

I was not Jackie Robinson. I knew I could not keep quiet

on the baseball field like Jackie because I am a talker and a social person. I wanted the Stars to accept me not only as an athlete but also as a human being, a person worth knowing. I didn't want them to think of me merely as a pitcher who could help them win games. I suppose it's the same way with many star ballplayers. I'm not saying I was a great star, but I wanted them to know me, not just my right arm. Most pitchers want to be liked for who they are, not just for what they can do with a baseball. I knew I had earned the Stars' respect on the field, but how was I going to gain their respect off of it?

I initially kept my mouth shut and observed everyone and everything. I wanted to be respectful toward them, and I hoped that they would, in turn, be respectful toward me. I grew to know my team, especially Mr. Sedberry, as we sat on the bench watching baseball for two seasons.

During that time, Mr. Sedberry and I learned to respect each other as we discussed sensitive issues, like race. I never dreamed I would talk to a black man the way I talked to Mr. Sedberry.

Much later, during the 1960 season, he told me that he had never dared to speak so openly to a white man. He said our conversations caused him to think about life from a different perspective, the white man's perspective, and sometimes our positions differed tremendously. Surprisingly, we also shared many of the same opinions and beliefs. Our relationship eventually developed into one that allowed us to conceive what the other side was thinking and to share those conceptions, and sometimes misconceptions, with one another.

Carl Sedberry, Jr., was born in Clifton, Texas, in 1933, and his father owned an auto body shop and café. The junior Sedberry grew up working in both, but he told me he liked working in his father's café better. Carl Sr. was a fine infielder who coached the local black baseball team. He loved baseball and taught the strategies of the game to his son, who didn't have his father's athletic abilities.

In 1947 the family moved to Graham, Texas, and the senior Sedberry opened a barbecue place on Lincoln Street called Sedberry's Café. At that time young Carl attended the one-room school for blacks, Lincoln School. Two years later the white principal of Graham High School met with the Sedberry family and explained to them that their son would be the right student to integrate Graham Public Schools. The parents pondered his request for some time. Probably scared to death of the situation, the son told his parents he simply did not want to go to school with all those white folks.

His parents did not force the issue. They decided that they could find a good school for their son without causing him a nervous breakdown in the process. That meant Carl Sr. drove for two hours every Sunday, taking his son to an aunt's house in Fort Worth so that Carl Jr. could attend Terrell High School (founded in 1921 and originally named Fort Worth Colored High School), an all-black school. Each Friday the father returned to pick up his son for the weekend. Junior returned to Graham after graduation to work at the Graham Magnetics Company and at his family's café, which he operated after his father retired.

Carl Jr.'s time in Fort Worth allowed him to experience life in a big city, coming into contact with many different kinds of people. Those contacts were useful to him when he became a baseball manager, dealing with other managers and players from various places, large and small.

In 1953 Mr. Sedberry began managing the Stars. The field

in Graham was initially just a sandlot ballpark. In 1957 the white community in Graham approached Mr. Sedberry with a plan to build a new baseball field on the Stars' sandlot, with upgrades including grass, lights, bleachers, fences, and concessions. City officials told him that if the blacks in Graham wanted to continue playing baseball on the lot, Mr. Sedberry's team would have to help build the new field. The officials also told him that the black community would not be allowed to use the new field on Sundays, when the white teams would play. Instead, the Stars would play on Wednesday nights, when the white baseball players were attending prayer meetings.

Black baseball fans and players in Graham worked on the field in the evenings until it got dark. They also worked on Saturdays, digging holes, welding, and stretching bull wire around the perimeter of the ball field. Mr. Sedberry was so committed to the project that he would continue working through the weekend, including Sunday, once the field was nearing completion. One Sunday his mother and father, driving home from church, spotted him, and his mother made his father turn the car around. She gave him a tongue lashing in front of his friends and led him by his ear to the car. He protested the entire way but returned home with them. Mr. Sedberry and his parents were happy that the white community ultimately remained true to its word and allowed the black team to use the new field on Wednesday nights, not even charging them for electricity.

Mr. Sedberry took pride in such small victories and always considered himself the team's manager, not its coach. He often told me that most of us knew more about how to play the game than he did. "Coaches will tell you how to improve your game," he said. "I don't do that. I will let you know where the next game is, what time it will start, when to be there, and how to get there. Organization is my strength. I also know who the best players are. Mainly, I just put those players on the field and let them play. Sometimes I have to let everybody play, though, to keep them motivated."

He provided us with organization and discipline. He kept a strict inventory of our equipment and hauled it to games. Our bats, balls, and bases were precious to him, and he knew where each one was at all times. He had a little black book that held all the names and phone numbers of the Stars and other semi-pro teams in the area. Every time we played a team, Mr. Sedberry would ask the manager for the names and phone numbers of other black teams, and they would share information. Then Mr. Sedberry would call the new teams to set up games, and they would all swap phone numbers again. If a team canceled, he'd find another game for us. He kept that book with him at all times because sometimes a few of the players, and sometimes whole teams, would need reminding on game days to come to the field.

Although he was extremely busy managing us, he always made time to compliment me when I performed well. He'd tell me, "You have an above-average fastball, but you have the best curve ball I've ever seen. You are so confident of your control that you can throw a curve on a 3–2 pitch and catch the batter looking for a fastball. You'd rather let a batter hit the ball than walk him. I've seen you average about one walk a game." He asked me to start every game for them on Sunday afternoons and Wednesday nights. "Three days' rest is all you ever seemed to need or want," he told me. I appreciated his telling me about my strengths, and his encouragement improved my game.

Our humble manager hauled our equipment, planned our schedule, and identified good players, but he would never admit that he was also an amazing coach. I knew he had baseball intuition. As he prepared the lineup for each game, he was especially gifted at knowing when to make substitutions. He was a gracious and pleasant man. I especially enjoyed watching his coaching style. He could feign ignorance when it suited him and then turn around and discuss sophisticated baseball strategy with me, privately and in some depth.

For example, Mr. Sedberry acted dumb and country when he disagreed with a call from one of the umpires. He would yell, "Ump, that wasn't a strike! The ball was over the batter's head!"

When the umpire defended his call, Mr. Sedberry would widen his eyes, open his mouth wide, slap his hands to the side of his face, and exclaim, "Sho 'nuff!" He would then turn to me and resume whatever serious conversation we were having, such as discussing the lineup for the next game.

The other Stars also liked Mr. Sedberry. Rabbit thought he was a great coach but knew of his one weakness. Mr. Sedberry couldn't bat. Rabbit enjoyed laughing at Mr. Sedberry when we didn't have enough players and he would have to take his turn in the lineup, though that happened more often during the 1960 season than it did in 1959. Mr. Sedberry never wore a Stars uniform, even when he had to make an appearance at the plate. The absurdity of his wearing a dress shirt and pants while batting made Rabbit laugh even harder at him when he took a swing.

Mr. Sedberry would subject himself to such ridicule because, most of all, he loved the game. He studied it closely and was an excellent strategist. His skills had paid off when he asked me to join the Stars. Somehow he knew that I was the missing piece of a successful ball club. Mr. Sedberry had seen all the black ball clubs in West Texas and knew there were not any top black pitchers available. He and catcher Alfred Ray probably didn't recognize how tremendously innovative their scouting of the white Oil Belt League was. Yes, Mr. Sedberry and Alfred were bold, but they had no other source of pitching. The isolation of West Texas forced them into the situation. A more populated area might have offered them more black prospects, and my services would never have been needed. In an era in which asking a white man to play for a black team would have been considered foolhardy, Mr. Sedberry and Alfred found me.

If I've been called "Jackie Robinson in reverse," then Mr. Sedberry can safely be called "the black Branch Rickey." Numerous ballplayers, both black and white, always referred to Branch Rickey, the white president and general manager of the Brooklyn Dodgers who signed Jackie Robinson, as "Mr. Rickey," just as I showed respect to Mr. Sedberry by using his last name. Years later Rabbit told me how he also held Mr. Sedberry in the highest regard. "I always respect a man for his ability. We weren't calling him Coach Sedberry. We called him Mr. Sedberry," Rabbit said. Mr. Sedberry earned Rabbit's respect not as a player, but as a manager. Some players would argue that a manager needs to have played the sport to be any good at managing a team, but Rabbit recognized Mr. Sedberry's great baseball mind and organizational skills. Mr. Sedberry was the heart of the Stars.

Similarly, major-league players respected Mr. Rickey because he not only organized and ran the Dodgers but also created a farm system that grew talented players for the major-league team. Mr. Rickey scouted Roy Campanella, who played in the Negro Leagues, as early as 1945. He, Stan Musial, Buzzie Bavasi, Dick Williams, Al Gionfriddo, Duke Snider, and Bobby Bragan all called their boss "Mr. Rickey"

(Bragan and Guinn 1992). They admired him greatly. In fact, Bobby Bragan, who was born in 1917 in Birmingham, Alabama, played with Jackie Robinson in Brooklyn and credits him and Branch Rickey for helping him end his belief in racial segregation (Bragan and Guinn 1992).

Mr. Rickey had decided long before he signed Robinson in 1947 that the Dodgers needed stronger players to win games. He saw the untapped talent in black players, and like Mr. Sedberry sending Alfred to scout me in the white Oil Belt League, Mr. Rickey sent his scouts in search of talented players in the Negro Leagues. Both men wanted to win baseball games, and to accomplish their goals they desired the most talented players, no matter what color they were. Their desire to win baseball games and willingness to integrate their teams caused immeasurable changes in the hearts and minds of those around them.

Mr. Sedberry's amazing vision of an integrated Stars team led to wins at home and in Abilene against the Blues, but we were about to be tested on a longer road trip. The crowds in Wichita Falls and Abilene did not seem offended by my presence. The Stars fans had been especially supportive of my appearances, so I hoped a few of them would travel to our next game and ease my nervousness about traveling out of state. As we prepared to travel to Grandfield, Oklahoma, to play the Zebras, Mr. Sedberry told us the Zebras would be the best team we would face that summer. He was right.

We packed players and equipment into three full cars, eventually arriving at Grandfield in the southwestern part of Oklahoma. The ballpark was at the end of a long, narrow dirt road, where we could see close to a thousand people waiting in the distance. As we approached them, we realized many members of the crowd were extremely short because the local black population included some people with dwarfism.

A small wooden stand at the entrance to the ballpark displayed admission prices, but we almost drove by it because we didn't see anyone in the booth. Suddenly, a dwarf with a hand-held stop sign appeared in the booth and screamed, "Halt!"

Wayne Fisher, our first baseman, was sitting in the first car on the front passenger side. He laughed and said, "Hey, shorty, you'd better stand up or nobody will see you!"

The little guy was, in fact, already standing on a chair. He yelled back, "I am standing up, you smart-ass!"

Wayne's feet, propped up on the dashboard, floated above the dwarf's head when we pulled past him and into the parking lot. Wayne had some of the biggest feet I had ever seen. Unfortunately, he had broken his left foot while working his regular job as a concrete finisher in Wichita Falls, and the foot had not healed properly. It pointed at an awkward angle.

Despite his foot, Wayne was a physically imposing teammate, 6'4" and very muscular. He batted and threw left, and he played first base well. That position was responsible for covering a smaller part of the field than, for example, a center fielder. First basemen are traditionally tall but not fast, built to stand, stretch, and catch balls that are thrown to first. Wayne fielded ground balls and threw with equal dependability. As one of our two powerful left-handed hitters, he was a gentle giant, always cheerful and kind. I liked him because no matter what the situation, he was in a good mood. He never cut up, but he did smile a lot.

As we approached the stands, we noticed an overflow crowd had started parking along the left- and right-field foul lines. The field had no outfield fence, and I suddenly felt very enclosed by the strangers surrounding me on the field. I became more dependent on my new teammates for their support than I had at home games. I trusted that they would help me feel comfortable.

Mr. Sedberry then got out of his car and started searching for the Zebras' manager. When he couldn't find him, he asked a circle of tall Zebra players for help. The players widened their circle to reveal their manager with dwarfism, Nero, sitting down in the middle of them, going over the lineup. He looked like a miniature Redd Foxx.

He was a feisty little man, and he yelled at Mr. Sedberry, "I'm down here, damn it! What do you want?" He was wearing a very small Zebra uniform. Instead of vertical pinstripes, the Zebra uniforms sported alternating horizontal one-inch stripes of black and white material. "Zebras" was stitched in black across a white stripe on their chests, and each player also had his number in black on his back along with the name of his spouse. I wondered if the names on the zebra-striped uniforms deterred any potential girlfriends. The black and white stripes shifted around Mr. Sedberry, and we laughed as Mr. Sedberry bent down to talk to the manager.

We became quiet, though, as we watched the Zebras go through their warm-ups. I knew I'd have my hands full. Their pitcher was the best I'd seen or would ever see in the West Texas Colored League. The crowd, which included a large entourage from Wichita Falls and Graham, had started an early celebration in the stands, drinking and talking to each other. As we warmed up, I'm sure the Oklahoma fans noticed I was white, but they did not seem to care. They wanted to watch a ball game, and they were very happy to cheer for us, regardless of our color.

After seven innings, we became locked in a pitchers' duel, 3–3, when, with two outs, Nero decided to put himself in the game as a pinch hitter. He crouched down as low as he could and presented a strike zone of maybe twelve inches. I walked him, but the next batter hit a sharp grounder deep in the hole between second and third base. Our shortstop, Earnest "Fat" Locke, fielded it cleanly and easily threw Nero out at second as he headed toward the bag with little waddling steps. Our crowd couldn't help but laugh as the tiny manager ran toward second base. I have no idea why the Zebras didn't use a pinch runner in that situation. Nero's ego probably prevented him from substituting another player for himself. Or maybe he thought the batter at home plate would hit a home run. Either way, his not assigning a pinch runner to first base probably cost him the game.

Still tied at the top of the ninth, down to our last two outs, Mr. Sedberry called timeout and put in big Hubert "Bo" Beasley as a pinch hitter. Bo was another concrete finisher from Wichita Falls, and he enjoyed playing left field for us, batting and throwing left, and occasionally delivering towering home runs. At 6'3" and 250 pounds, he wasn't fast, so Mr. Sedberry's choice of him as a pinch hitter surprised me. Our manager's intuition paid off, though, and Bo hit a fastball so far that it rolled past the crowd and into a stock tank, a small pond used to provide cattle with water. The crowd went wild as Bo danced to first then second base, taking bows. Baseballs were expensive and valuable to both teams, but no one wanted to push past the cows gathered around the stock tank and wade into the water to retrieve the ball. Mr. Sedberry laughed as the Zebra outfielders stood at the stock tank's edge, peering into the dark water. Nero, still upset about his performance on the field, didn't want to order anyone to get the ball. We all stood around, waiting for the umpire to make a decision. I thought that maybe the call would be a ground-rule double.

Before a call could be made, the frustrated Zebra center fielder dove into the tank, retrieved the ball, and nearly threw Bo out at third. Without an outfield fence, the ball was still in play even when it was under water. Mr. Sedberry ran out on the field and argued violently that it wasn't the same ball. He wanted the umpire to rule the play a home run and give the Stars a one-run lead.

"Hell," he hollered at the umpire, "that could be any ball! Who knows how many balls are in that tank!"

The Grandfield umpire inspected the ball and declared that it was the same ball that Bo had hit, or close enough, and the tied game continued with Bo looking dejected at third. The ruling was ridiculous, but what could we expect from a Grandfield umpire?

Wayne Fisher was the next batter, standing oddly at the plate with his one big foot askew. He worked their pitcher to a 3–2 count and then hit a little opposite-field blooper to put the Stars ahead 4–3 as Bo lumbered across home plate, this time not stopping to dance or take bows. I retired the bottom half of the ninth for the Stars' win.

Mr. Sedberry offered immediate congratulations to me for my victory, but my new teammates were a little slower to acknowledge it. They had been understandably wary of me during our first games together. After our win against the Zebras, they started to warm up to me. During our next few games, they began telling me how I should behave to be more like a Star.

Fat, the shortstop, was the first Star to offer me his opinion. He liked me, but, then again, Fat liked everyone. Most of all, Fat admired lovely ladies, and they seemed equally enamored of him. He was tall and slim and had a pencil moustache. He once laughingly told me, "They call me Fat because I was a fat baby, but I turned into a very handsome man!"

Fat looked a lot like a young Leroy "Satchel" Paige, who had pitched beautifully in the Negro Leagues, primarily in the 1930s and 1940s for the Kansas City Monarchs, and then in the major leagues for the Cleveland Indians (1948–49), the St. Louis Browns (1951–53), and the Kansas City Athletics (1965), where the fifty-eight-year-old ended his career as the starting pitcher on September 25. Amazingly, he threw three scoreless innings, only giving up one hit, a double to Carl Yastrzemski in the top of the first. He batted once in the bottom of the second inning and struck out against the Red Sox's Bill Monbouquette. I thought Fat was nearly as talented as Satchel, and Fat thought so, too. I enjoyed watching the graceful and quick Fat play shortstop. He had a great arm and was just as good at batting and stealing bases. He had played minor-league ball with the Oklahoma Black Cardinals and the Wichita Falls Spudders. When the Kansas City Athletics first offered him a contract after the integration of Major League Baseball, his wife, Catherine, would not leave Texas. Fat stayed with her in Wichita Falls, played for the Stars, and later drove a city bus. I imagine his bus rumbling down the city streets, radio tuned to a baseball game that he would be participating in if only she would have agreed to move.

Fat would pitch on very rare occasions if I needed relief. If we played an even rarer doubleheader, we could sometimes convince him to be our starting pitcher. He was a fine pitcher, but he preferred playing shortstop because he could talk when he was at that position. As the team talker, he found that batters didn't appreciate his talking to them from the mound. Talking to a batter will unnerve him, possibly make him angry, and even cause a fight. While fielding, batting, or pitching, Fat constantly insulted the other team, but he really wasn't interested in starting a fight.

Black teams then were notorious for hurling racial epithets at each other. I had no idea how to react the first time Fat stood up and shouted a degrading insult at our opponent's pitcher. The pitcher had charged off the mound to field a little broken-bat dribbler and tripped, embarrassing himself as he fell.

"What's the matter, nigger? Did you trip over your lips?" Fat shouted at him.

Then Fat turned to me and said, "Now, don't you ever say that, white boy!"

My standard answer after glancing at the all-black crowd became, "Fat, do I look suicidal?" This comment would always cause my teammates and a few of the front-row fans to laugh.

Fat's fielding and vulgarity, though masterful, were far surpassed by his womanizing. Fat had an old Chevy convertible, black with a black leather interior and a black top. Naturally, he drove with the top down and the front seat always occupied by a lovely lady. When we were playing out-of-town games, Fat never allowed anyone else to carpool with him. During those games, we'd be sitting on the bench, and Fat would be waving to his lady.

"Fat," I'd ask, "is that your wife?"

"No, white boy, that isn't my wife," he'd say. Although the women were always different, his answer was always the same for two years. A few years later, his wife, Catherine, divorced him and moved to Denver. As a single man, Fat could finally leave Texas, but by then his best ball-playing days were behind him.

My comical exchanges with Fat encouraged the others to talk to me, but I really don't know when their acceptance of me became complete. It was gradual, as it should have been. Conversely, the crowds that attended the games and followed the Stars accepted me much more readily because they liked to win. I don't mean they liked for us to have more runs at the end of the game. That was good, too, but they liked to bet money, lots of money, on us.

I was amazed by the amount of money that changed hands each game. My first year with the Stars, we lost only one game, and the fans were very happy with me, especially the ones who were gambling. The gamblers adored me for my part in their winnings. In Grandfield, I saw fans exchanging an entire week's wages on the outcome of our games.

I once asked the other players how the fans collected bets at a rival team's field. I learned it was a very simple process. At away games they only placed bets on who would win. The fans would then ask an elderly man or woman whom they trusted and couldn't run too fast to hold the money. Still, around the eighth or ninth inning, the bettors were keeping their eyes on their money. I don't believe any of the old folks ever got away.

Before we left Grandfield, I experienced my first away-game tailgating party. My teammates' wives always rode in separate cars, except for Fat's always-absent wife. The Stars brought the beer, and the wives brought the food, especially an abundance of home-cooked fried chicken, which we always shared with the opposing team.

We sat on truck tailgates, on bumpers of cars, or in folding chairs when they were available. Mostly the men visited with the men, and the women visited with the women. Sometimes small black children would stand near me, staring. We were never in any hurry to leave. Tailgating was very pleasant, something I had never experienced before because white ball clubs always shook hands after a game and then left for home. I learned to look forward to the Stars' after-game camaraderie with opposing teams.

Mr. Sedberry remembered when we played away games the fans from Graham would drive out toward Lattermore's beer joint by Possum Kingdom Lake and buy three or four cases of beer. "Fat and the Wichita Falls boys would do the same," he told me. "They bought the damndest brands of beer we ever did see. I guess they was real cheap because they tasted like they was. Seems like they prided themselves on bringing brands we had never heard of each week! I liked to drink Pearl and Schlitz back in those days. I tried Jax, but it always gave me headaches."

At the Grandfield tailgating party, my nickname of "white boy" changed in a significant way. Wayne Fisher had a number of friends and relatives in Grandfield, and he introduced me all around. He would put his arm around my shoulders and say, "This is *our* white boy, Jerry."

The significance of Wayne's introducing me to his family and friends as "our white boy" and using my first name was apparent to even an unsophisticated country boy like me. I was touched. I had become "their white boy." Before I was simply "white boy," but now I was becoming a part of the team, and Wayne's friends and family knew my first name.

We played Grandfield again the following Sunday at Spudder Park. Fans started arriving at noon for the 2:00 p.m. game, and Mr. Sedberry looked happy with the number in attendance.

"Well, Mr. Craft, I estimate we have about fifteen hundred in the stands," he said. "Let's not disappoint them."

We didn't. We were tied 3–3 in the top of the ninth. The

Zebras had runners on the corners with one out. The batter hit a grounder deep in the hole to Fat's right side. Fat fielded it smoothly and threw to second. Emmitt Johnson tagged second and relayed the ball to Fisher at first for a close double play. The runner was safe.

Mr. Sedberry protested mightily, but to no avail. The run scored, and we trailed by one going into the bottom of the ninth.

Two outs later all hope seemed lost, but Rabbit hit a double to right field. Bo Beasley was up next, and we cheered for the two-out rally. Bo hit the first pitch to deep center field for the final out. We had just lost the game, our last opportunity to play the Zebras that year. Mr. Sedberry said that neither team would schedule another game because no one wanted to lose again. Our 4–3 loss to Grandfield at home was our only loss of the 1959 season, my favorite with the Stars.

After our games against Grandfield, I started to feel that the Stars had accepted me, but we faced the challenge of playing more away games, sometimes in hostile environments. Mr. Sedberry would call me a day or two before a road trip and tell me where to meet so we could caravan to the opponent's town. We had to carpool because someone always needed a ride. Various cars would not be running, or sometimes one would be in the shop. Team members would get a ride from a neighbor to the meeting point. We met in Jacksboro at the courthouse if we were headed south or southeast. If we were traveling to Oklahoma, we met at Spudder Park in Wichita Falls. Trips to the west started at the courthouse square in Graham. When we ran out of gas or had a flat tire, we'd make room for as many players as possible in the next car.

Each road trip was an adventure. The jokes, songs, and

discussions and comparisons of women were always enlightening. My team could really sing well—blues, rock-and-roll, and gospel music. They would harmonize and shout, "Oh, yes!" During the trips, I gravitated toward the teammates who were the kindest to me.

I always brought my 1958 bronze Chevrolet Impala convertible, and I welcomed whoever joined me. Usually Rabbit, Alfred, and Bo rode with me, but that arrangement sometimes changed because we never knew who would need a ride.

When we were all assembled, Mr. Sedberry led the way in his car. Many of the luxuries we take for granted on road trips now were not available in those days. We had no fast-food restaurants and no food "to go." Instead, we each took our own sack lunch and ate it on the road. We brought fried chicken and homemade roast beef sandwiches because they weren't messy and didn't spoil easily. When we got hungry, we stopped at gas stations that served whites only, and I went inside to buy the entire team cold drinks and chips while my teammates waited outside.

My teammates did not seem upset by this arrangement. I think they were happy that I was along so that they could have cold drinks. They were a real luxury for my team. Because segregated gas stations were a fact of life, my teammates were appreciative that I was willing to get their drinks.

We got plenty of rude stares during those stops at gas stations, but I don't remember anyone asking me what I was doing. Really, to even the simplest redneck, I was obviously a part of a team. We were all wearing uniforms, so observers knew we were going somewhere to play baseball. I never parked my car out of sight. That would have been insulting to my teammates, as if I didn't want to be seen with them, despite the hostile looks from store owners and their white patrons.

Even the most prejudiced of store owners didn't mind taking my money, so boycotting these establishments on behalf of my friends would not have made sense. In fact, the whites-only gas stations were usually our only way to get gas and food when we were on the road.

We sometimes tried to avoid stopping at gas stations by topping off our tanks before we left town. There simply weren't as many gas stations as today, and we took our chances on running out of gas every time we passed one. I don't remember any stations refusing to sell gas to me for our team, though they could have easily done so.

I soon learned that road trips with the Stars could be fun. Rabbit didn't drink, but the rest of the guys usually had a couple of beers on the way, more for a longer trip. During those road trips, we would have to stop to use the rest room, especially if we brought beer with us. Those stops were complicated because blacks could not use the white public rest rooms. Instead, we'd have to pull down a side road or a country lane.

One of the players in Mr. Sedberry's car at the front of the caravan signaled us to stop by holding his cap out the window. We carefully chose abandoned country lanes because we couldn't risk being reported to the law. If the trip was really long and the beer flowed, we'd make many of these side trips. It's no wonder we were always late for games.

Once we stopped, we placed lookouts at the end of the country roads. If they spotted a car coming, they yelled, "Bottoms up, boys!" Every once in a while, a lookout would cry out a false alarm, which caused a lot of ribbing and laughter as my teammates struggled with their pants.

On the road trips I got to know Clarence Elbert "Rabbit" Myles, who is still my good friend. Although he could have fun, he was a serious competitor and the most reliable of my teammates. Small but strong, Rabbit had been an outstanding quarterback in his hometown of Halletsville, Texas, where he was born on April 5, 1935. As a child, he played his neighborhood's version of baseball with tennis balls and broom handles. That was all they had for equipment.

His all-black school used wood-burning stoves for heat, and on cold mornings the students had to bring the wood inside from the wood pile stored under the building. The school had no coaches or a gym. Instead, the school's principal organized games against football teams from Edna, Cuero, Gonzales, Seguin, and Luling. Rabbit's football team had to mow the weeds and fix their own football field, which was really just a cow pasture.

During basketball season, their high school team's practices were held outside on dirt courts. When his team asked to practice inside at the white high school, they were told they weren't allowed in the gym. Rabbit's coaches knew better than to ask that their regular games be held inside. The same outdoor dirt practice courts hosted their games, leaving players and fans uncomfortably exposed in cold weather.

When Rabbit was sixteen, a local semi-pro baseball team spotted him playing football and recognized his athleticism. The baseball team's manager asked his mother if he could join their team. His mother thought he was too small to play, but the team convinced her, so he played with them in the summer. That was the first time he had played real baseball with standard balls, bats, and gloves.

Rabbit's great-grandparents had been slaves, and, as Rabbit told me, "My grandfather carried a lot of hatred in his heart for white folks but knew he had to make his living off them." Rabbit's grandfather and namesake, Clarence Louis Gartley, had no education. He never knew how to read or write, but he could do basic math. He never owned a car. Instead, he drove a horse and buggy. Clarence often told Rabbit that life wasn't always fair to a black man, but he could still have a good life.

Rabbit remembered his grandfather telling him and his friends how to handle themselves in public. When they went out, they tried their best to avoid trouble and used back doors when entering businesses. Their strategy was to avoid confrontations and not be stopped by white men when away from home. When a white man disparaged Rabbit's group of friends, they would leave. Rabbit had a few white friends, too, so he realized that not every white man felt the same way about segregation.

Clarence told Rabbit, "Carry yourself well, have a good attitude about yourself, always associate with your own race, and then with just the right people. Avoid people with bad habits, whether they are black or white." Despite his grandfather's advice, Rabbit decided to give friendship with me a chance, and I soon respected his play in center field and his ability to transform pitchers' fastballs into towering home runs.

He and his wife, Arnita Campbell Myles, opened a construction business in Wichita Falls in 1960. He still runs it, and he's still my friend and the friend of countless others he coached in basketball, football, and baseball over the years at the Boys' and Girls' Clubs there. Rabbit continues to have a standing invitation to fish at my ranch and bring his Boys' and Girls' Club children, too. Years ago he brought Fisher, Fat, and Mr. Sedberry to fish, but now only Rabbit and I are still alive. Back then we talked about the old days with the Stars, drank some beer, enjoyed the country, and cleaned the fish. When Rabbit is in Jacksboro, he'll stop at my office. We visit and have lunch together. I still think he's a great guy.

Rabbit says he's been satisfied with his life, though the thought of being born a little later and making a living playing professional baseball does cross his mind. He tells me he was happy to have played three years for the Stars. He played because he loved the game, never earning a cent. He remembers the little money the Stars made from admissions went toward equipment or travel expenses. Rabbit never worried about the Stars' lack of funds. He had a great attitude and knew how he wanted to live and treat people. He's been married fifty years and raised three boys. The black and white communities in Wichita Falls respect him, and he can become reflective about his years there.

According to Rabbit, the black communities of Jacksboro and Graham in 1959 and 1960 accepted my playing for the Stars, but Wichita Falls was different. Fewer people in Wichita Falls knew my family, so the people there were more suspicious and skeptical of me. I knew, however, that Rabbit would always come to my defense. I considered Rabbit my friend, and my fondness for him caused me to trust him completely, even enough to allow him to pitch for me once in a close ball game.

One Wednesday night we were playing an away game against the Hornets of Aspermont, Texas. Aspermont is a small town located thirty-two miles west of Haskell on Highway 380, about a hundred and fifty miles west of Graham. The Stars had a small lead in the bottom of the ninth inning, but the Hornets' cleanup batter was coming to the plate. Rabbit trotted in from center field and asked me for the ball.

"I want to pitch. That guy's good, and I'm tired of him mouthing off to me," he said.

"OK," I said. "But if this guy gets on base, I'm coming back in to pitch." I handed the ball to Rabbit.

I went to second base, but Rabbit waved everybody in. "Go to the dugout and stack up the bats," he said to them. "This game is over." The batter, bewildered at the absence of fielders, struck out on Rabbit's curve ball.

While Mr. Sedberry, Fat, and Rabbit got to know me and like me, Bobby Lee Herron was always an enigma. He was sixteen years older than I was, born Robert Lee Herron on March 13, 1924, in McKinney, Texas. Although he was thirty-five years old when I was his teammate on the Stars, he was still an extraordinary athlete. Bobby never seemed to accept me, though. He never adopted "our white boy" as a term of endearment for me.

Perhaps it was his professional experience that set him apart from us. Records from this time are sketchy but indicate that Bobby Lee Herron, known as "Big Daddy" or "Big Bob," was born in McKinney, Texas, and later played fullback for Booker T. Washington High School's 1943 state championship team. He also played baseball for the 1950 Houston Eagles and the 1951 New Orleans Eagles of the Negro American League's Western Division and for the 1959 Detroit Stars. In 1959 Ned Powers of the *Saskatoon Star Phoenix* reported that Herron spent a "highly productive season in the ranks of the Kansas City Monarchs" and "was selected to play in the East-West all-star game at Comiskey Park."

On Stars game days Bobby always wore his old Monarchs uniform, which had blue short sleeves and an open collar. Both shoulders displayed patches with a large "KC." The rest of the uniform was light gray, including the long-sleeved blouse that was trimmed with two cords of blue piping running from the shoulders down around the button placard. "Monarchs" was stitched in large blue letters in print, not script, across the chest. His pants were a matching shade of gray, and his stockings were blue. His cap was gray with blue cording and a blue bill with "KC" on the front to match his shoulder patches. The whole ensemble was quite distinctive, awing us and his opponents. Obviously, it left an impression on me. Even then, I knew I was looking at history.

He once told us that his hero was his old Monarch teammate, Leroy "Satchel" Paige. Nobody doubted that Bobby had played with Paige, but Bobby offered few details about his days with the Monarchs. We never thought to engage him in conversation or ask him if his baseball travels ever took him to Mexico with other black players who couldn't play on white teams in the United States. Now he's gone, and the record is too incomplete to confirm if he ever played baseball south of the border. I couldn't even imagine asking him about his former teams when we played on the Stars together. We were simply never that friendly toward one another.

Bobby always sat on the far left-hand side of the bench, rarely conversing with anyone. After the level of baseball he played, perhaps Bobby felt he'd lowered himself by playing with the Stars.

I also assumed that Bobby didn't care for me because I was white and therefore an intrusion. Years later, though, Rabbit and Mr. Sedberry assured me that Bobby didn't particularly care for anyone.

I believe that many gifted athletes like Bobby have difficulty dealing with life after their glory days. Decades after our days as Stars, I would stop for breakfast with Fat and Rabbit at the IHOP restaurant in Wichita Falls on my way to my ranches in New Mexico. We updated each other on our jobs, our families, and our sense that the next generation, both black and white, lacked our work ethic. We also talked about our baseball days. During one breakfast, Fat became uncharacteristically quiet. He was probably not feeling well, and I asked him what was wrong. He started reflecting on his past.

"Well, life didn't turn out like I thought it would," Fat replied.

"I don't think it ever does, Fat. I think the way we accept our lives and the choices we make truly build our character," I said. He smiled at me, knowing we'd been teammates a long time ago and were friends now.

Bobby probably felt that same disappointment during his time as a Star. He played right field and was an imposing figure, standing about 6'4" and weighing between 230 and 240 pounds. Now that I think about it, most of my teammates were taller than I was, which is why I remember them all being about 6'4". We were a very impressive group when we were traveling together. It's probably for the best that I left them in the parking lot when I entered gas stations; otherwise the attendants might have felt a little intimidated by the height of our group.

Bobby was a very reliable fielder and still had a good arm, but I could tell it had once been great. He would occasionally blast a towering home run, awing the other players and fans and giving us a glimpse of what a tremendous player he had been. I wonder what records he could have shattered in the major leagues if he had been allowed to play at that level when he was younger. Although Bobby was only twenty-three when Jackie Robinson broke the color barrier, there were far fewer major-league teams then, and the minor-league system that supplied them was loaded with talent. He, like many black players of his era, would have had to wait for a very long time to begin a career playing in the majors. I never asked him why he didn't try to become a major-league baseball player, playing instead for several Negro League teams and one season with an all-white minor-league team in Texarkana, Texas.

As the least social of the Stars, Bobby wasn't exactly ugly or rude to me. He just kept to himself, mentally and physically, though he mellowed a little with age. After retiring from baseball, he worked as a building superintendent for the Maskat Shrine Temple in Wichita Falls, Texas. Before Bobby died in 1994, he, Rabbit, and I sat in the dugout at the Jacksboro High School Baseball Field for an interview with John Pronk from Channel 8 in Dallas. For the first time I heard Bobby reminisce, as old ballplayers tend to do, about his days with the Monarchs in the 1950s. He also said that Fat reminded him of Satchel Paige in that Satchel was a constant talker and "baiter" of opposing batters. When Satchel wasn't pitching, he would do his best to distract the other team's batters by making funny or rude comments to them. When he pitched, his irritating windup was equally distracting to the batter. He would pump his arms back and forth a number of times, extend his body backwards, close to the mound, stick his big left foot in the air, and somehow come uncoiled with a blazing, hidden fastball.

Bobby also said that Satchel and Fat looked a lot alike, and they did. When he was finished talking, I pointed out that just as in his days with the Stars, Bobby was still sitting away from the rest of us, on the far end of the bench. We had a good laugh about that. We also laughed remembering Mr. Sedberry's attempts to give the Stars the sign for bunt.

During our first season together, I told Mr. Sedberry that our team should try something new. We should learn to bunt.

"I think it's a real detriment to our team that we never bunt or flash signals to the batter or runners, like 'take' and 'steal,'" I told him.

"Well," he said, "white teams have more discipline. I know when we should bunt, but I can't get anyone to do it because all your teammates want to do is hit home runs."

We had a team meeting and agreed we needed to bunt. We worked on our first sign: touch your ear, cap bill, then belt buckle.

During the next game, we tried our new strategy, but Mr. Sedberry got excited at the start of the game and either forgot or confused the signs. He flashed a signal to Bobby, who was the first batter, and so began our grand experiment. Bobby had one foot out of the batter's box, watching Mr. Sedberry perform a confusing gyration of signals.

Finally Bobby stepped completely out of the batter's box and yelled, "Damn it, Carl, just tell me what you want me to do!"

Bobby was no stranger to confusion on the baseball field. He once told me that during his first season with a Class A Texarkana team, he became the first black man to play for an all-white, East Texas minor-league team. Opening Day festivities at the brand-new stadium included the mayor of Texarkana throwing out the first pitch. Miss Texarkana, a stunning blonde who waved and beamed at the appreciative hometown crowd, also attended. She came as part of a contest: the first Texarkana player to hit a home run on Opening Day would be treated to dinner at the local country club, escorted by Miss Texarkana herself. Bobby batted number five in the lineup, and with one man on base in the sixth inning, he hit a home run.

The crowd rose to its feet, but as Bobby rounded second,

waves of silence broke over them, and they sat down. Bobby stopped near the shortstop position to find out what was wrong. The crowd had realized that a black man had hit the first home run of the season. Guess who was coming to dinner! Looking toward the stands, he saw that Miss Texarkana had fainted in the arms of her father. Her mother was pointing at Bobby and screaming. Realizing the implications of his home run, Bobby sprinted to home plate and then into his dugout, absolutely terrified.

Timeout was called, and the teams' owners, coaches, and umpires conferred at home plate. After an animated conversation, the only logical conclusion was reached: Bobby was called out for missing second base. He later told us, "Damn, man. They took away a home run from my stats because of that white woman. And why in the hell would I have wanted to eat with any white woman? Good Lord, they would have found me hanging from the tallest pole in Texarkana the next morning." Bobby knew his own team had taken his home run off the scoreboard rather than allow him to have dinner with a white woman.

Bobby also remembered that most hotels would not allow him to stay with his white teammates. And even if he had been allowed to stay in the white hotels, who would have been his roommate? So, accommodations were arranged for him on the other side of town, where the black hotels were.

He couldn't even get to the ballpark the same way his teammates did. His white teammates took the team bus from their hotel to the ballpark, but Bobby had to catch a cab from his separate hotel to connect with the bus. Sometimes the cab took him directly from his hotel to the ballpark. Once, when he finally arrived at a ballpark, he learned the town had passed laws preventing blacks from playing there.

Bobby especially disliked the isolation of separate dining and socializing after games. He felt hostility from both races when he played for white teams, which induced his ambivalence about the benefits of integrating baseball. He found that when a town allowed him to play, black fans disliked him because he was playing with a white team rather than in the Negro Leagues. Even Mr. Sedberry termed players like Bobby "traitors to their race," believing that no matter how talented the black ballplayers were, the majority of those who signed with a white team would never make it out of the minors and join a major-league team.

Nevertheless, with the best black ballplayers gone to the major leagues, it was the beginning of the end of the Negro Leagues, a loss that Bobby and Mr. Sedberry mourned deeply. Mr. Sedberry told me that he deeply regretted the demise of what he called "black ball" and that he thought the white major-league clubs had bought all the good black players and "warehoused" them in the minors, paying them less than they had earned in the Negro Leagues. He thought many talented black players had little chance to advance to the major leagues with white players stacked in front of them. With their players organized in such a way, major-league teams could claim they were integrated without ever having to advance black players from the minors to the majors. He believed white owners used this method to eliminate the Negro Leagues.

While Bobby remained emotionally reserved around me, most of my teammates, like Fat, Fisher, and Rabbit, had accepted me. However, our team was still missing a close camaraderie that most teams enjoy. A road trip to Waco, Texas, gave us a shared, though traumatic, experience and common ground that connected us all.

The Southwestern Bell African American History Month
Family Day and Negro League Baseball Reunion (Southwest)
at the African American Museum in Dallas at Fair Park
on February 20, 1999. From left to right are
James Williams (who played for a different
team managed by Mr. Sedberry), Jerry Craft,
Mr. Sedberry, and Jerry's teammate
Clarence "Rabbit" Myles.

Jacksboro's Old Town Team, circa 1931. Left to right
in front row: Masters Randolph and Bert Noel, bat boys;
second row: J. D. Craft (Jerry's father), Harry Key Turner,
Jess Massengale, Claude Gregg, Peck Wade, Shine Myers,
Pat Patoosis; back row: John K. Hackley, Pete Simons,
Chet Brummet, Darrell Lester, Wallace Myers
(Jerry's future high-school baseball coach),
Red Stoddard, and Bones Risley.

Jerry Craft's thirteenth birthday party in 1950 with his baseball friends. Left to right in front row: Linda Craft, Nick Sikes, Jerry (holding the cake), Jim Boley, Richard Teague, and Tony Clark. The back row includes Keith Patton and Don Massengale.

Jerry Craft in 1953 on the Jacksboro High School football team. Helmets at that time did not have facemasks, and the injury to his left eye, from playing with a pocketknife as a child, is clearly visible.
Courtesy Jacksboro High School, Jacksboro, TX.

Jim Boley, Bobby Murray, and Jerry Craft, the tri-captains of
the 1954 Jacksboro High School football team. Each Jacksboro
player picked his own number, which confused opposing
offenses and defenses. The 1954 team became the 9AA
District Champions. No yearbook photos exist of the
baseball team because the baseball season started after
the deadline for printing the yearbooks.
Courtesy Jacksboro High School, Jacksboro, TX.

J. D. Craft, center, winning a cutting horse
championship in 1955 at the Will Rogers Coliseum in
Fort Worth, Texas. He and his favorite horse,
Miss Texas, have just been named champions
of a cutting horse contest at the Fat Stock Show.

Jerry Craft's high-school graduation photo in 1955.
He and 54 other students graduated that year, earning the
nickname "55 in '55." Jerry was an honor graduate
and president of Jacksboro High School's chapter
of the National Honor Society.
Courtesy Jacksboro High School, Jacksboro, TX.

Monroe "Mo" Henderson fielding a baseball as
shortstop for Texas Tech University in spring 1957. He
was varsity baseball team captain at Texas Tech during
the 1956 and 1957 seasons and a three-year
letterman (1955, 1956, and 1957). His batting
average his senior year was .346.
Courtesy of Monroe Henderson.

The 1959–60 All-College Football Champions of
Texas Tech University, Sigma Alpha Epsilon Fraternity,
with Jones Stadium in the background. Left to right
in front row: Jerry Craft, Bob Tinney, Delbert Bassett,
Warner Phillips, Jack Lalament, Malcolm Garrett,
Dick Phelps. Back row: Jimmy Johnson,
Daryl Summers, Bob Kinney,
Jerry Pearson, Jimmy Williams,
and Gordon Richardson.

Jerry Craft representing his cable television business partner and Texas State Senator Tom Creighton in Newport, Texas, in 1965 at a campaign rally. The event was a "tri-county speak-in" for all the Democratic candidates in the three counties surrounding Newport.

Linda Craft with her golf clubs in 1983. She was a member of the LPGA from 1967 until 1973. She and Penny Zavichas created the Craft-Zavichas Golf School in Pueblo, Colorado, in 1968 to help women learn to play golf. The school is still in operation.

Earnest "Fat" Locke and wife, Catherine (Cat), on their
wedding day. They were married in June 1951
at the Mount Calvary United Methodist
Church in Wichita Falls, Texas.
Courtesy of Sandra Contreras.

Earnest "Fat" Locke in his bus driver uniform. He drove a bus for the city of Wichita Falls, Texas, from January 1999 until his death on July 30, 2004. Previously he was a salesman at Nunn's Electric in Wichita Falls until his retirement in December 1998. Courtesy of Sandra Contreras.

Clarence "Rabbit" Myles and wife, Arnita, on their wedding day on May 30, 1959. They were married in Graham, Texas, at the home of Arnita's father, Mr. James Campbell. Courtesy of Clarence Myles.

Coach Clarence "Rabbit" Myles and his basketball team for
the Boys and Girls Clubs in Wichita Falls, Texas, in 1981–82.
On the front row, second from left, is his son Elbert; front row,
fourth from left, is his son Melvin; front row, far right, is his
son Clarence, Jr. Rabbit coached Boys and Girls Clubs
teams for twenty-nine years, touching hundreds
of young lives. Courtesy of Clarence Myles.

Carl Sedberry at the Dallas African American Museum in 1999 at a reunion of former players. He appeared on a panel under the theme "Triumph Over Adversity" narrated by historian Larry Lester. Courtesy of NoirTech Research, Inc.

Eddie Klep, on the right, was the first white American widely known to play in the Negro Leagues. Klep played briefly for the Cleveland Buckeyes in 1945. Here he is pictured in his Rockview Prison uniform from his 1951 stay. Courtesy of NoirTech Research, Inc., donated by Ethel Klep and Dr. Alice Carter.

Dave Hoskins eventually joined the major leagues with the Cleveland
Indians in 1953. A year earlier, Hoskins became the first
African American to sign and play in the Texas League with
the Dallas Eagles. He was the leading pitcher on the team
with twenty-two wins and ten losses.
Courtesy of NoirTech Research, Inc.

Jerry Craft spent two years as a pitcher for the Wichita Falls/Graham Stars
as the first white player in the West Texas
Colored Baseball League. Photograph by Gary Lawson;
originally published on the front page of the
Wichita Falls *Times Record News*
(November 23, 2005, vol. 99, no. 165).

Jerry Craft and wife, Pamela, celebrating
Thanksgiving with family on the Craft Ranch
in Jacksboro, Texas, 2006.

FIVE
Welcome to Our World, White Boy

WHEN MR. SEDBERRY ANNOUNCED a July 1959 road trip to Waco, Texas, to play the Tigers, I turned to Fat and said, "Hey, this is our fourth weekend on the road. Spudder Park is, by far, the finest stadium in the league, and our fans always come to see us play there. Why are we always on the road? Why lose our home-field advantage?"

"White boy, we know everyone in Wichita Falls," he said. He looked at me like I was a moron. "We like to travel to play baseball so that we can meet new people."

This concept startled me. When I played white semi-pro ball, I didn't socialize with my teammates, the other team, or their fans. After the game, we shared a handshake and sometimes nodded our heads toward one another. That was the extent of my postgame conversation with my white teammates and the other team.

The Stars, on the other hand, looked forward to socializing at away games, beginning with our ride sharing. Mr. Sedberry organized four cars—his, Rabbit's, mine, and Fat's—for the Waco trip. On our way out of town, we stopped at Bobby Evans and Paul Brotherton's Sporting Goods Store on Ninth Street in Wichita Falls. During the season we bought all of our baseball equipment there, including bats, balls, caps, uniforms, shoes, and catching gear. Both owners had played sports in college, and after graduation in 1954 they had opened their store together in the segregated section of town, the east side.

Wichita Falls was divided, black and white, not by an official municipal policy but by history, tradition, and geography. The south, north, and west portions of the city were exclusively white, including Wichita Falls High School. Nicknamed "Old High," the 4A school featured a powerful football team.

The "wrong" side of the tracks lay to the east, where the black community lived and worked. Booker T. Washington High School was the "Pride of the East Side" and the equal of Old High in athletics, although they never played one another. The white community in Wichita Falls would not have tolerated being defeated by Booker T. As no other large, all-black high schools existed in Wichita Falls and north into the Texas Panhandle, Booker T. played in an all-white 3A district against Brownwood, Childress, Iowa Park, Bowie, and Henrietta. These smaller schools could suffer defeat more easily than the venerable Old High. Booker T. was particularly difficult to beat at home because every black person within walking distance of the games attended them. Those games were easily one of the east side's greatest sources of community pride. The school produced several Division I college athletes, but most had to play in California or in the Big Ten Conference because many Texas universities were still segregated.

Bobby Evans, whose sporting goods store is now located on Kemp Street in Wichita Falls, still remembers supplying all of Booker T.'s and the Stars' athletic equipment. After we made our purchases and left Bobby's store, the caravan to Waco began. About an hour outside of town, Mr. Sedberry's car broke down. The frustrated players piled into two cars, mine and Rabbit's. Fat was also driving, but his front seat was occupied by his latest lady friend, and he wanted no additional passengers. The ride was terribly uncomfortable, people and equipment stuffed everywhere, but we had no choice. No white mechanic would work on a black person's car on a Sunday, or probably any other day, and we knew no black mechanics nearby. We left the broken-down car by the side of the road and hoped it would still be there when Mr. Sedberry returned, black mechanic with him, to either fix it or have it towed.

We arrived in Waco more than an hour late. The heat and crowded traveling conditions caused us to be in a foul mood. When we found out we were playing on a very recently used cow pasture, we felt even worse. Only the black community used the cow pasture baseball field, and no one could afford to maintain it. Dry and not-so-dry piles of cow manure decorated the infield dirt. I looked around with wide eyes as we unloaded our equipment, but Mr. Sedberry just shrugged at me. We found shovels and paper plates, and both teams scooped the manure off the infield as if it were part of a regular pregame routine.

The rest of the field lacked baseball's usual amenities. I noticed right away that the infield did not have a pitcher's mound. Instead, an ancient pitching rubber sat directly on the flat ground. The edges of the rubber crumbled into the dirt. Three benches along the infield fences served as our dugouts. Our players rested on the benches, but we had no protection from foul balls.

Once we had cleared the infield, I walked toward the outfield. I didn't get very far because giant weeds, at least two feet high, stretched into the next county. No outfield fence stopped them, and I did not understand how our outfielders were going to chase down fly balls under those conditions. The Stars would have no way of seeing rocks or holes and could fall or twist their ankles very easily. I wondered how we'd find a fly ball if a player didn't catch it or if it rolled past him. For the first time I felt relieved to be a pitcher, even though I had no mound and only a fragile piece of rubber marked where I should stand. After I inspected the outfield, I followed my team to the benches. Despite the condition of the field, I looked forward to playing a team I had never faced before.

More than five hundred Waco fans also anticipated the game. Our car trouble had delayed the start of the game, but the crowd didn't care because that meant they had extra time to drink. The fans laughed and joked with each other, feeling very festive as they sat around the edges of the cow pasture on warped bleachers. A few sections of them had rotten or missing planks, causing unexpected gaps in the crowd.

Because the field had no bullpen, I walked across the infield to the rotting pitching rubber to begin my warm-ups. The first time I stood on the rubber and pushed off, it tore apart.

"Mr. Sedberry!" I yelled and pointed to the broken pieces at my feet.

"Whoo boy!" he characteristically proclaimed. Mr. Sedberry's favorite expression in critical times was always "Whoo boy!"

"What else can go wrong today?" he added. He shouldn't have asked.

He waved to the Tigers' manager and explained the problem. The manager, a very large, pleasant man, filled every inch of his oversized uniform. The manager then called the Tigers' team captain to the broken rubber.

"I have a tool box in my trunk with some hammers and long bridge nails," he said, handing the captain a key. "We'll get this thing fixed."

"What is this 'we'?" the captain asked. "I is the captain, and I don't do that sort of thing. You fix it yourself!" He gave the key back to the manager.

The manager instantly stood toe-to-toe with the captain and announced, "I is the manager. I give the orders on this team. Now, you go get that toolbox!" He shoved the key back in the captain's hands.

"I AM NOT YOUR NIGGER!" the captain screamed back as he ran to the car's trunk, unlocked it, and grabbed one large tool, a combination hammer and hatchet. "I AM GOING TO KILL YOUR BLACK ASS!" He let out a scream and ran toward the manager like a Comanche with his tomahawk drawn back.

Mr. Sedberry and I stood back with our mouths open as the very large target of a manager ran for his life. The captain swung at his head and just missed. Then the Stars all sprinted for the safety of our benches. We stood behind them to view the fight.

The fans delighted in the unexpected entertainment. Cries of "Kill him!" arose all around us. The crowd started placing their bets, and the safe money seemed to be on the faster Tiger, the one with the weapon. As the two combatants circled the bases, I told Mr. Sedberry, "My God, he's trying to kill that man! Shouldn't we call the sheriff?"

"Good grief, Mr. Craft," he replied and stared at me in disbelief. "Do you really think the police would drive out to this cow pasture on a Sunday afternoon to keep black folks from killing each other?"

I could see his point.

Our attention returned to the field, where the fight continued. As the manager and the captain started around the bases a second time, the captain tripped over first base, fell, and lost his weapon. The manager, now exhausted, grabbed a bat and screamed, "Now you better move your black ass!" He swung at the captain's head, but the smaller and quicker captain ducked.

They started their third trip around the bases, this time with the manager in pursuit of the captain. The bets in the stands started to shift to the manager. "Kill him! Kill him!" the crowd again chanted. With all the betting, we felt as if we were back home.

After they ran the bases two more times, both fell exhausted. The appreciative audience brought them beer, and, after a short rest, the manager and captain started repairing the pitching rubber together like nothing had happened. To the Waco fans, the fight had been part of the afternoon's entertainment.

The Stars then started to relax and talk among themselves

freely, but I really didn't want to stay in Waco after seeing the Tigers nearly kill each other.

"Mr. Sedberry, why don't we just go home?" I asked. My initial excitement at facing a new team had faded in the heat and hostility.

"No, we traveled all the way here, and the fans want to see a game. We should play," he replied.

I slowly nodded my head, but I had been distracted by the fight. My mind wasn't on pitching, and the Tigers jumped out to an early lead. In addition, our usually reliable outfield was peculiarly inept, showing no hustle. They moved slowly through the tall weeds and made odd little hops when they walked from the outfield back to the bench. Between innings I asked Rabbit what was wrong with the outfielders.

"Snake holes," he replied.

"Snake holes?" I asked.

"Yep, all over the outfield. We are scared to death of rattlesnakes," he said.

As we took the field for the next inning, I called timeout and asked Mr. Sedberry to join me in the outfield. We stepped through the tall weeds, and I explained to him what was distracting his players from catching fly balls.

"There," Rabbit pointed. "There's a snake hole." Mr. Sedberry and I stared at what looked to me like an armadillo hole. The holes are quite common in the Texas countryside.

"Ah, Rabbit," I said. "That's just an armadillo hole."

"How do you know the difference?" he asked.

"I'm a country boy," I said. "I know." But he continued to stare at the hole from a safe distance.

"Well, country boy, do rattlesnakes sometimes live in armadillo holes?" he asked.

That was a good question. I hesitated. "Yes, they sometimes do," I said reluctantly. He glared at me, but I quickly
added, "I'm quite sure no snakes live in those holes." The
crowd was becoming impatient with our team meeting and
hole inspection.

"If you're so sure no snakes live there, you put your arm
in that hole," Rabbit taunted. Mr. Sedberry and the outfielders waited for me to check the holes, but I declined. The
crowd began booing us loudly, and I feared the possibility
they would become more hostile if we didn't get the game
started again soon.

"Let's do our best to keep the ball in the infield," I told
my teammates. I returned to the mound and told the infield,
"I'll pitch the ball low, so watch for ground balls."

Amazingly, we won that game despite our extremely slow
outfield. We concluded that we didn't want to stay for our
usual postgame visit with a crowd of drunks who enjoyed
watching violence. We were not comfortable in Waco, and
we made plans to return home.

Mr. Sedberry suggested we load up quickly and have supper in West, a small town north of Waco founded by Czecho-
slovakian immigrants. On our way to West, we started chat-
ting about the game. The Tigers chasing each other with a
hatchet, the snake holes, and the hostile crowd had been
enough for one day. We didn't know that our day was about
to get worse.

I asked Mr. Sedberry if any of the restaurants in West
would serve our team. "We're going to a black café, Mr.
Craft," he laughed. "I've eaten there several times."

When we finally arrived at the small café, a white frame
house with a big front porch that faced the railroad tracks, we

were very tired and hungry. Our team eagerly anticipated an unexpected treat, sitting down together and ordering a good meal at a public restaurant.

I dropped off my teammates at the door and parked the car. Because of the heat, they didn't wait for me. They went into the restaurant and ordered huge amounts of food.

When I walked in several minutes later, I noticed some of the black diners staring at me, but I thought little of it. Sometimes I got stares when I was with my teammates, and I had grown accustomed to them. I sat down with the Stars and looked over the menu.

The Stars continued their discussion about the game, and they teased me again about the snake holes. I was happy to be included in their conversation.

As soon as I started to relax with them, the owner of the establishment quickly came over to my table, leaned over, and said softly to me, "Sir, I don't want any trouble, but you are going to have to leave."

"Why?" I asked.

"Because you are white, and my customers don't want you here," he said.

At first Mr. Sedberry ignored the exchange and asked me why I hadn't ordered my food yet. I tried to respond to Mr. Sedberry, but I was interrupted.

"We're not going to serve this man," the owner told Mr. Sedberry.

Mr. Sedberry was instantly out of his seat and at my side, protesting as if the restaurant owner were an umpire who had made a bad call. "This man is a member of my baseball team," he told the café owner. "We are hungry, and he is trying to place an order."

"It don't make any difference who he is," the owner replied. "He is white, and he has to leave. The rest of your team can stay."

"We are a team! We play together as a team, we travel together as a team, and we eat together as a team," Mr. Sedberry responded indignantly. He was in shock because he never expected such treatment in a place that had always been friendly toward him and the Stars.

Rabbit remembers that Mr. Sedberry "kind of went off his rocker" at this point. All the food the team had ordered was arriving at the table, and we were really hungry. Mr. Sedberry looked at all the plates of food on the table and looked at me. I couldn't believe what was happening. Rabbit couldn't believe it either.

Rabbit later told me that he was just as surprised as Mr. Sedberry. He explained the situation to me this way: "I could understand if you'd been a black man going into a white restaurant because I'd seen that happen when I lived in San Antonio. You couldn't get served in a white restaurant if you was black. The black man had to go in back doors to get something to eat." But he'd never seen a white man refused service anywhere.

Mr. Sedberry then took a deep breath and turned away from the owner. He sat down again and said calmly, "Let's eat," to me and the team. He truly wanted his hungry team to eat. That strategy was not going to work. The owner would not back down.

"Not here you won't!" he yelled.

"If Jerry doesn't eat, then we don't eat!" he yelled back at him. Mr. Sedberry turned toward the door and clenched his fists. I had never seen him so angry. To a man, my teammates stood up and walked away from plates full of food. The door was slammed and locked behind us. The owner decided to turn me out rather than make good money off a team of hungry ballplayers. He would rather waste that food and lose money than serve a white man.

I stood in the bright Texas sun, stunned, trying to comprehend what was happening to me. Bobby Herron walked up beside me, put his left arm around my shoulders, and with a rare, large grin said, "Welcome to our world, white boy!"

I realized that Bobby was delighted to see a white person endure the humiliation that he and his teammates had endured for years. Alfred Ray nodded in agreement with Bobby. Alfred alone had the presence of mind to rescue his can of beer from inside the restaurant and was sipping it thoughtfully. Suddenly, he jumped and threw it into Rabbit's car. I looked around to see what had made him throw away his beer. A West police car rolled into the parking lot. The café owner, fearing retaliation from our team, had called the authorities.

The cop was a stereotypical small-town southern law-enforcement officer of the late 1950s. He knew we were trouble, and he was going to keep his jurisdiction safe.

"What you boys up to?" he asked, using the word *boys* in exactly the way my teammates hated it. We slowly backed toward our cars.

"We're leaving, sir, just like the man asked us to," I told him.

"What you doing with these niggers?" the cop asked, looking me up and down.

"I play baseball with them, sir," I said.

"I bet your folks are real proud," he smirked. He stepped over to Rabbit's car, leaned on the window, and said to Rabbit, "Well, boy, I can see you've been drinking."

"No, sir," Rabbit said. "I don't drink." Rabbit had been trying to read a map, plotting the fastest route out of West, maybe through Hico and Weatherford. He put the map down and looked up at the police officer.

"That's a beer can by your foot, boy," he said, pointing and smiling.

I tried to explain Alfred's recently discarded can. "Oh, the guys in the backseat had a few after the game, and it must have rolled out from under the seat when we stopped to eat." The cop completely ignored me. He reached into Rabbit's car and grabbed the can.

"Get out," the cop told Rabbit.

"Get out for what?" Rabbit asked.

"This beer is cold," he said.

Rabbit glanced away and said nothing.

"Get out. You are drinking beer," he said.

"No, I already told you. I don't even drink," Rabbit said.

"Well, the can is in the car with you," he said.

Rabbit pointed at Alfred. "He threw it in the car with me," Rabbit said.

"No, you get out," the cop said again.

Then Rabbit got angry and started talking. If he hadn't said anything, he might not have been arrested, but talking to a white cop meant he would go to jail.

"Boy, I'm going to have to arrest you," the cop said to Rabbit, and he handcuffed my friend and took him to jail. That was the first time Rabbit had ever been arrested. The Stars were stunned. We saw the patrol car drive away, Rabbit in the backseat. He glanced sheepishly at us, probably knowing he shouldn't have said anything.

We couldn't leave our friend in West; we had to get him out of jail before we went home. His wife certainly would never let him play with us again if we returned without him, and we knew we would never find a better center fielder. We started searching our pockets, bags, and car seats for spare change.

We didn't have much money, but we gathered everything we had, probably a little less than fifty dollars, and went to the jail. Mr. Sedberry and I asked if we could pay Rabbit's fine.

"How much do you have?" the jailer asked. When we told him, he said that wasn't enough.

"It's all we have," I explained.

"I guess we'll have to leave him," Mr. Sedberry added as we backed away.

It was a risk, but Mr. Sedberry knew they didn't want Rabbit. They wanted to take our money and to scare us away.

"Well, I guess that will do," the jailer sighed, as he stuck the cash in his pocket and unlocked Rabbit from his solitary cell. "Now, I don't want to see any of you boys around here ever again. We don't have room in our jail for an entire base-ball team," he said.

His message was clear, and the Stars never returned to West. We drove home broke and hungry. I was still in shock as I traveled back to Jacksboro with my silently starving teammates.

I'd never seen the Stars so quiet, so subdued. The long, difficult trip to a game in a hostile environment followed by the humiliating incident at the restaurant in West and Rab-bit's unfair arrest caused our silence. On the way home, we did not stop for gas, breaks, or food because we had spent all of our money bailing Rabbit out of jail. We were emotionally exhausted, and the team never discussed the Waco trip again.

The Stars endured and accepted humiliation daily. I was

often surprised at their lack of bitterness toward whites and was embarrassed that my teammates were often treated terribly. They accepted that this was the way it had always been and would always be.

A few days after my trip to Waco with the Stars, Jacksboro had a long late-afternoon rain. Rain in West Texas always puts ranchers in good moods, especially a summer rain, so my father and I decided to sit on the front porch together and enjoy the weather. We sipped iced tea while my mother fixed supper.

To my surprise, my father asked about the game in Waco, and I told him about the snake holes. Encouraged by his interest in my team, I told him what happened after the game.

"Then I got kicked out of a black restaurant in West, and one of my teammates got arrested," I continued. That was probably too much information for my father. His mood instantly turned indignant.

"Why, the nerve of that black son of a bitch to tell my son to leave! He had no right to kick you out of there!" he said.

"Well," I said, "until then I never felt much of anything when the TV showed blacks forcibly removed from public places. Now I think I understand in a tiny way the resentment they feel because I was the one being rejected."

"But blacks shouldn't be in places set aside for whites!" he said.

"Evidently I was in the wrong place, too," I said. Then I quietly added, "Don't you imagine that black fathers feel the same way when their sons are dragged out of public places?"

He stared at me for a minute, and then we sat in silence. "Can I get you another iced tea, son?" he finally asked. He stood up and walked to the kitchen.

Even with his back to me, I could tell that he had softened

slightly. He may not have agreed with me or how I was spending my summer, but as a father, he understood a man's desire for his son to be treated fairly. His reluctance to continue the argument meant that maybe he was considering my perspective. My mother always said that the Craft men's vocabulary never included, "I could be wrong," or "I'm sorry." My father's silence on the matter was as close as I would ever get to those words.

When he came back with my drink, the conversation turned to major-league baseball, something we always enjoyed discussing. He loved the game and knew team statistics much better than I did. I studied the newspaper's sports page so I could talk to him about baseball. We discussed every aspect of the game: pitchers' records, stolen bases, batting averages, RBIs, and home runs.

My father's hero was Mickey Mantle. Many rural Texans at that time felt the same way because Mantle was a country boy, a native of Commerce, Oklahoma. My father identified with him. After Mantle retired, he bought some ranchland south of Jacksboro, and my father had a chance to meet him. The real-life Mantle, however, did not fulfill my father's expectations of a hero. He told me that Mantle had evidently been drinking heavily, and his speech was slurred. My father, who never minced words, came to the conclusion that Mantle was "a smart-assed drunk."

After learning about Mantle, I was glad my heroes were Sandy Koufax and Whitey Ford. My father and I listened to the Yankees play the Dodgers on the radio, rooting for one team and then the other. My father particularly loved the antics and homilies of Casey Stengel and Yogi Berra. They were giants in that incredible era of baseball.

Mostly, however, we talked about the pennant races. I eagerly anticipated them and the World Series because even the ranching chores were put on hold during those games. We watched our favorite teams, the Yankees, Dodgers, and Red Sox. My father, strangely enough, viewed the black ballplayers in the same statistical category as the white players, meaning that if they played well enough, then they were OK. If they did not perform well, then racial slurs were almost always added to his critique of them. Despite the slurs, he was slowly accepting black athletes if they were competent baseball players, and I knew this was progress for him. I was witnessing progress in all of us, but it didn't come rapidly or easily.

Six
Calf Fries and Home Runs

WHILE MY FATHER AND I SPOKE IRREGULARLY and briefly about the Stars, the other members of my family, my white friends, and neighbors tried to avoid the subject, especially as I became accepted by the Stars and continued traveling with them. My father and mother were the only members of Jacksboro's older white community who ever spoke with me about the team. My white friends asked me a few questions from time to time, but I don't think they really understood what I was doing. The neighbors probably talked incessantly about my situation among themselves, but not with me or my family. The gossip entertained the entire community.

My father, on the other hand, hated gossip. He was an outspoken and prejudiced man, but at least he was not afraid to say what was on his mind. In retrospect, he may have disliked my black teammates and their influence on me because he always wanted to be in control. For example, he never had a cup of coffee because he thought he'd be unable to control himself around it. He told me it smelled so good that it must be addictive, and he refused to become addicted. He proclaimed, "Too many Jacksboro ranchers sit around in Hatty's Café or the Green Frog Restaurant drinking coffee and bullshitting when they should be out working!" If he thought a person should do things differently, meaning his way, he would relentlessly express his opinion.

My father's friends often remarked that they didn't understand how my sister and I could have such strong wills given his controlling nature. He wanted to control our lives, and instead of breaking us, he made us more stubborn than if he had given us our freedom. I think that my strong will was a direct result of my fighting constantly for control of my life. When I was with the Stars, my father had absolutely no power over me. Playing for the Stars was something I could do apart from him, knowing that he probably would never see me doing it. I didn't have to worry about his attending my games, evaluating my play, or arguing with me after the game about my abilities or errors. We would probably have fought much more often if he had attended the Stars games.

My mother avoided such clashes. In fact, I don't remember my mother saying she opposed my playing on a black baseball team. It didn't make a lot of difference to her. She could see that I was happy, and I'm sure there were more important matters keeping her busy. She did what was expected of most housewives during that era by cooking three meals a day, keeping house, and tending children. On Wednesday afternoons she practiced playing the organ for the Methodist church, and on Thursdays she attended bridge club. My mother, sister, and I went to church on Sunday. My playing baseball did not affect her routines.

If any of my white friends were bothered by what I was doing that summer, they didn't mention it to me. They probably didn't care. We had graduated high school in 1955, four years earlier, and we no longer spent a lot of time together. Many of them had already married and left Jacksboro. They had done what we always said we wanted to do: get out of our small town.

Sometimes, though, my white friends who stayed in Jacksboro would see me in my Stars uniform at the root beer drive-in on Live Oak Street. They would ask, "Who are the Stars?" and "Where are you playing this summer?" I explained to them that the Stars were a black baseball team, and we played throughout West and Central Texas, and sometimes even in Oklahoma.

"Why are you playing for a black team?" they asked me.

"When we were younger, we played baseball with Jacksboro's black kids. What I am doing now really isn't much different, though we are a little older," I explained. "It's like pickup games for adults, though having a league makes it a bit more organized." Then my friends smiled, nodded, and said nothing more about it.

However, their parents, like my parents, may have questioned my participation on the team. After all, my playing with the Stars was no secret in Jacksboro. There are no secrets in small towns.

I imagine the conversation around our neighbors' supper tables: "Why do Jay and Lou Craft allow their son to pitch for that black baseball team in Wichita Falls? And he really seems like such a nice boy. Probably going off to college did that to him!" But the neighbors never asked me in person about my activities or my team. They simply would not have discussed the team with me in their polite circles of friends.

During my first summer with the Stars, a good friend and Texas Tech fraternity brother Malcolm Garrett of Clovis, New Mexico, came through Jacksboro with his wife and young son. They called to say they wanted to see me. I readily agreed, but I told them I'd be playing ball that night. I invited them to see me play in Graham. I also told them the circumstances of the team and game. To my surprise, Malcolm agreed to bring his family, including his young son, Skip, to see the Stars.

Going home after the game, Malcolm told me that his wife was initially frightened during the game. She had said to him, "Malcolm, I've never seen this many black people together in one place. I'm afraid for us and little Skip. Let's leave."

"Jerry would not have brought us here if there were any danger. I trust him," he had told her.

Malcolm said they were treated very kindly during the game. The black fans from Wichita Falls and Graham could easily guess that the white spectators were my friends because there were no other white people in the stands. The regulars welcomed them, saying, "You must be here to watch Jerry. Good to have you."

I was happy but not surprised to know that Malcolm and his family enjoyed the game and eventually felt comfortable watching me play. Malcolm said to me, "I guess I'm embarrassed to say this, but I never shook a black person's hand before tonight."

As much as I enjoyed having my friends at the Stars game, it made me realize that my father had never watched me play and probably never would. A few times during those years, I felt his absence. Perhaps my need for him to see me play and to approve of my baseball skills outweighed my need for independence. If I urged him to watch us, I knew the answer would always be "no." Perhaps he felt the absence too, but, like nearly everyone in his generation, he didn't approve of the races mixing, even on a ball club.

I knew he would decline an invitation to see the Stars because we would occasionally get into arguments over race, and his opinions were very different from mine. After we ate supper one night, I remember watching a television newscast with him while my mother cleaned the kitchen. The news featured a story about a community beach. Blacks were not allowed to use the beach, and they had gathered to protest their exclusion from public property.

"Look at that! I think everyone should be allowed to use that beach because it's a public beach," I blurted out. Boy, that started it.

"Blacks should not be allowed to use public facilities because they don't own anything. If you don't own anything, you don't pay taxes, so you're not paying for your share of the swimming pool, or playground, or beach," he said.

"Sure they own homes. You know that. You've seen them. Why do you look down on the black race?" I pointedly asked him.

"Hell, everybody needs somebody to look down on. It makes you feel superior!"

"If that's so, then who do the blacks look down on?" I asked.

"Probably the Mexicans," he answered.

"I believe anyone with your point of view is very insecure," I said.

Our voices were rising, and my mother remained silent until things became really heated. She shouted at us from the kitchen, "That's enough! Both of you shut up!"

That worked. She knew she couldn't change her husband's opinion, and I think she might have secretly supported mine. Maybe she hoped that over time my generation's way of thinking would replace hers. Ultimately, her thoughts didn't matter because my father worked me twice as hard on Stars' game days, usually until the time I needed to leave for the game.

Before each game I showered, shaved, and put on a clean uniform. The ballplayers of my day arrived at the stadium looking their best. When I watch games today, the players look like they haven't shaved in days. They need haircuts, too. Maybe they think facial hair, curls, chains, and earrings are intimidating, but Mr. Sedberry would not have allowed them on his club.

Mr. Sedberry always admonished us before we played a white team about our personal appearance and demeanor.

"Look your best. Be your best," he said. "Be proud of yourselves. Don't give the white folks any reason to say that the Stars are dumb, country niggers."

Whether we were proud of our team or afraid of white teams, the Stars behaved quite differently when we played them. Our usual raucous behavior would have easily incited riots among white teams and their fans. When we played an all-white team, particularly at their home field, we maintained a constant friendly chatter among ourselves but rarely insulted the white players.

I think the Stars were also a bit more subdued when I was around. Rabbit later told me, "You know, we wouldn't use profanity as much if you was in our presence. We would watch our language. I guess we all respected you. Among ourselves, we didn't care what we said. We might say anything." According to Rabbit, none of the Stars was easily offended.

When I played with the Stars, we just played our game and didn't complain the way today's players do. Pitchers now have sore arms. I never had a sore arm. My arm got tired after sixteen innings, but never sore. No matter how hot the day, I always wore a white, cotton long-sleeved jersey to keep my arm warm.

Working on my father's ranch kept my arm strong. Sometimes I'd arrive at the ballpark completely worn out, feeling as if I couldn't pitch two innings, and then I'd pitch a brilliant game. Other times, I'd arrive fresh, rested, and raring to go, and then I'd just get bombed. I sometimes wonder if the mental side of the game made the difference at those times. Some days I had what it took, and some days I didn't.

Either way, I always approached each game the same. I would be positive, poised, and confident. I don't think I was ever arrogant, certainly not when I was playing with and against black ball clubs. They had plenty of arrogance already, and I think neither the opponents nor the Stars would have tolerated or accepted any arrogance from a white boy, no matter how talented he was. They did not have to. Yes, they liked winning, but ultimately they would have enjoyed their games and social interactions without me.

As a Star, I had the most trouble playing against the white semi-professional team from Granbury. Many of them were my old rivals from state high school playoff games, primarily left-handed hitters who played baseball at Baylor University. With so much power from the left, they beat us twice in the 1960 season. A better fastball or a screwball would have helped me against them, but I didn't have either. My only real defense was my unusual dropping curve ball. A regular curve ball comes to a right-handed hitter from the inside and breaks toward the outside of the plate, but the same pitch is no mystery to a left-handed hitter. For a lefty, the dropping curve ball comes from the outside and breaks inside. He can watch it all the way. My dropping curve didn't challenge Granbury's left-handed batters. They were the only team I couldn't dominate.

Mr. Sedberry would play any team, anywhere. He once got a call from the manager of a team from Eastland, the Hombres, who were all Hispanic. Their manager had heard we were really good, so he told Mr. Sedberry the Hombres were undefeated and wanted to host us for a series of games. The Hombres were not an official member of the West Texas Colored League. Instead, they were a group of regular recreational ballplayers. Mr. Sedberry agreed and scheduled our first game against them on a Sunday in June at Eastland in 1959.

We had been instructed to be on our best behavior against white teams, but black teams and Hispanic teams were fair game for the rudest insults I'd ever heard. I think both races considered the other to be inferior. For the most part, no love was lost between the Stars and the Hispanic baseball teams we faced.

Compounding the volatile situation was the Hombres' undefeated season, but we soon discovered that the team was not as good as its record. We beat them quite handily, deriding their lack of playing skills and humiliating them on their home field. Fat, as usual, led the barrage of insults from the Stars' bench. His most exuberant vocal supporters were Bo Beasley, Vernon "Puddin" Higgins, and Sam "Bam" Brown.

The four of them drove the other team crazy. Quite frankly, those particular players could also get on our nerves.

Once the racial slurs started, no one could stop them. If our team laughed, the insults grew more personal and intense. As hard as Rabbit and Mr. Sedberry would try to calm the four clowns, sometimes they were so ridiculously funny that our leaders laughed along with them.

Black teams instantly responded by shouting their own insults from across the diamond. The jawing was always quite creative, but we all understood that no one wanted to start a real fight over the verbal exchanges. In fact, if a shouted insult was particularly creative, both teams and the fans joined in the laughter. It was simply a part of the game. At times the game seemed secondary to the insults because the arguments became more interesting than the action on the field.

While this behavior was readily accepted by the black teams and their fans, the Hispanic players did not appreciate a black team insulting them in front of their fans, particularly if the black team was beating them. That alone was insult enough. Add to that the machismo of athletic confrontation, and the situation could become volatile. Several times we came close to fistfights with Hispanic teams, but Fat and his group did not understand the danger of this situation or care to. Playing the Hombres, I could see a confrontation coming.

When an Eastland batter would make the sign of the cross as he stepped to the plate, Fat would yell out from his position at shortstop, "Yeah, you better pray for some help 'cause you sure ain't gonna see this next pitch!"

"You boys is undefeated? Who you been playin'? The Sisters of the Blind?" Bo chimed in.

The Eastland team became very resentful, especially when they witnessed the end of their undefeated season at the hands of the Stars. After the game, their players and fans followed us to our cars. We could tell they were cursing, not congratulating, us in Spanish.

One of our fans pulled a knife, which prompted several of the Hombres' supporters to do the same. Back then and still today many ranchers carry knives as work tools, but I was suspicious about our fans needing knives. I was worried that the Hombres and Stars fans were carrying knives for one deadly reason.

Luckily, Mr. Sedberry's trunk was open, and we grabbed bats, drawing back to swing if we had to. As we held the crowd at bay, we jumped in our cars and got the hell out of there, rocks hitting our rear bumpers as we drove away. My teammates' cars had souvenir dents from the game, but, luckily, the rocks missed mine. The Stars didn't seem to mind the dents. The group of players in my car laughed and cut up about the incident for miles. I didn't think it was so funny.

Part of the reason for the laughter may have been the adrenaline kicking in after such a close escape, or perhaps the Stars knew they had not been in any real danger because we were able to flee the scene quickly, unlike the time Rabbit was arrested in West. Rabbit could have spent many months in a jail cell, but in this situation we were on the road home in a few minutes. The lively drive from Eastland to Jacksboro was entirely different from the silent drive home from West.

"They can sure throw rocks better than they can throw baseballs!" Rabbit laughed.

Eastland's manager called the next night to see what time we would play the following Sunday. Mr. Sedberry refused the Hombres' invitation, which infuriated their coach. He felt insulted that we were not giving his players a chance to beat us in a rematch and regain their honor. I appreciated Mr. Sedberry's refusal to host the volatile, incompetent Hombres. As much as Mr. Sedberry loved scheduling games, the Hombres were much more trouble than they were worth.

The other all-Hispanic team we played was the Wichita Falls Lobos, who, like the Hombres, were not members of the West Texas Colored League. They were a good defensive team for a group who played regularly on the weekends, but they lacked pitching and power hitting. I hit my only home run in Spudder Park off them. There was no one on base, and I knew that I had hit the ball very hard, but couldn't follow the flight of the ball through the bright Sunday afternoon sky.

I ran hard around first, looked up, and saw their players looking down, kicking the dirt. I stopped halfway to second, assuming I had hit a foul ball. I started to return to the plate when the field official said, "Son, where are you going? You just hit a home run!" I sheepishly rounded the bases and entered the dugout to the laughter of my teammates. They knew why I had stopped before second base and talked to the official.

"Well, white boy, is it so rare for you to hit a home run that you forgot how to run the bases?" Fat asked. "Had to ask the umpire if it went over the fence?" My teammates told me the shot was just inside the foul pole, a 350-foot home run. I was proud of it anyway.

As a pitcher, I knew the pitchers I played against, and they nearly always threw fastballs down the middle to get ahead in the count on the first pitch. Pitchers still do this. I could never take the first pitch like batters do now. I don't understand why they look at that first pitch and get behind in the count. I always looked for that first-pitch fastball, loved hitting it, and did so quite successfully.

The following Sunday I hit two more home runs in

Granbury, both much longer, over their right-field fence. My friends were really ribbing me. "What you been eating, white boy?" they asked. "We want the recipe!"

"Oh, just a bunch of calf fries," I told them.

"What are those?" they wanted to know.

"Bull testicles."

They gasped, and I felt the need to explain further.

"When we work the calves at weaning time, they get branded and vaccinated, and the bulls become steers when we remove their testicles," I said. The look on their faces meant that I had given them too much information.

"All ranchers consider calf fries a delicacy," I continued. "We clean them, split them in two, flour, salt, and pepper them, and fry them. They are delicious!" My audience visibly cringed. "My father always told me that was one part of a calf the bankers couldn't take a lien on!"

"Man, white boy, how could you eat those things?" they wanted to know.

"I just do," I replied. I still do, with great gusto.

After briefly conversing among themselves, the Stars decided that eating calf fries wasn't worth it, not even to increase their home run production. Still, they had their fair share of homers, exclaiming, "Boy, I really shot him," every time one flew out of the park.

I remember the Stars' next road trip, my first time to play in Mineral Wells against the Fort Wolters Helicopter Base team. The U.S. Military and Mineral Wells have an interesting history. Fort Wolters began as a National Guard Training Center in 1921, but was renamed Camp Wolters and activated during World War II as an Infantry Reception Center, where soldiers received their basic training before being sent overseas. When the war ended in 1945, a group of local businessmen bought the camp and sold many of the buildings, using the remaining ones for light industry. The air force reactivated Camp Wolters in 1951 to train aviation engineers, who were sent to air force bases throughout the world. In 1956 the camp changed hands yet again when the army established a Primary Helicopter Training Center/School in Mineral Wells. In April 1957 the first graduating class had thirty-five members. Military personnel were very athletic on base, participating in basketball, golf, softball, and bowling.

When Mr. Sedberry called the recreation director at Fort Wolters to schedule baseball games there, he had to specify which team he wanted to play, the black team or the white team. Although the military had been integrated, the baseball teams at Fort Wolters were not. We would play both teams, but the black team was by far the better of the two. Our games were close, but the Stars always won. Their best player was 6'6" and said he'd pitched Triple A ball before being drafted into the army. He was the hardest-throwing pitcher I'd ever faced. However, he'd always throw the same speed pitch with no curve. I was patient, waiting to get runners on and staying close to the plate. One June night at Graham I hit his fastball so hard that I don't think it ever got higher than four feet off the ground, straight to right-center field, where it wedged into the bull-wire fence.

Bull wire is heavy gauged and tightly woven, two capital Vs facing opposite directions like acrobats supporting one another. It makes a good outfield fence because it's very strong when stretched and welded to metal cemented posts. Weaker chicken wire is better for backstops because it's lightweight, but bull wire is so strong it will turn back a bull, hence its name.

Their outfielders couldn't pull my ball out of the wire Vs. They stood there jabbing at it with their gloves until the umpires joined them. I had scored easily, but the umpires called me back to second for a ground-rule double. That was the hardest ball I ever hit. It may still be jammed into that fence. We left the ball there that night, and I don't recall anyone ever going back to get it the next day.

Sharing my secret recipe for home runs and then blasting one into the bull wire earned me greater respect among my teammates as a batter. I think the Stars were slowly changing the ways in which they thought about themselves, the game, their lives, and me. I realized this in late June, before a Sunday afternoon game in Abilene. My teammates from Wichita Falls had recruited a new player who was supposed to be really good. As I was warming up, I heard a commotion in the dugout. The new player, Harold, was fighting with Mr. Sedberry, Fat, and Rabbit. As a large crowd gathered, we watched Harold's baseball uniform fly onto the field.

Next came Harold, clad only in his jock strap. His car keys then landed at his feet, and he sprinted, his bare butt facing us, all the way to his car. The crowd cheered.

"What in the world was that all about?" I asked the group in the dugout.

"Harold didn't fit in," Rabbit said.

"What does that mean?" I said.

"Well," Rabbit replied after I pressed him, "Harold said some really bad things about you."

"Like what?" I asked.

"It doesn't matter," Fat said. "We won't put up with disrespect."

"I told you we'd always take care of you," Mr. Sedberry added. "You can count on that." And they always did.

• • •

During our first season together, we traveled to Haskell to face their black team, the Yellow Dogs. The team was named after and sponsored by a barbecue place west of Haskell called the Yellow Dog Tavern. Their team uniforms were white and had "Yellow Dogs" spelled across the front in yellow.

Rabbit remembers that particular game because he was injured while playing center field. A fly ball headed between center and left fields. "We usually call the ball in the outfield, but we didn't on that day," he told me. "Bo Beasley was playing left field, and we locked horns. We hit head-on. Both of us fell down on the field, and when we woke up, Mr. Sedberry asked us if we were OK. Wooden was all right because he was a really big man, but Mr. Sedberry took me to the bench.

"My head had a gash in it where we hit, but we didn't have much of anything to treat it with. We didn't have any money for first aid supplies. Mr. Sedberry found a bottle of rubbing alcohol. He asked me, 'Rabbit, can you handle it?' 'Handle what?' I asked. 'I'm going to put a little alcohol there,' he said."

Mr. Sedberry poured the rubbing alcohol on Rabbit's head, and Rabbit went out like a light. That was the second time he fainted that day, but he told me that his head wasn't sore after that.

We enjoyed playing Haskell because their baseball skills were good, but the food they shared with us after the game was even better. Their three or four competitive players were no match for the talent on our team. They couldn't beat us, but, boy, could they cook, and our entire team looked forward to the postgame meal.

The Tavern was about three miles away from the Yellow

Dogs' field. Both the ball field and the Tavern were equally run down, only the black community using them. We played Sunday afternoons on a cow pasture with no lights and no fence. In fact, most of the fields we played on had no fences. The runner simply had to beat the throw home for a home run. After a game on a hot summer day, I greatly anticipated driving the dirt road to the Tavern, thinking about cold beer and barbecue. As soon as I opened the car door, I could smell the brisket, ribs, and chicken from the smoker.

The Tavern's old unpainted frame building nestled in some large elm and cottonwood trees. Beneath them lay a few tables and benches, a collection of graying boards, almost skeletal in the bright sun. West of the Tavern sat the outhouse, a one-holer. When the wind was out of the west, as is often the case in Texas, we were reminded of the outhouse's exact location. The family that owned the restaurant and the ball club lived in the basement.

The Yellow Dog Tavern was comprised of one large room, connecting the kitchen and dining room. A large evaporative box cooler sat in a corner, making more noise than cool air. The tables and chairs were constructed of old two-by-four lumber, and the worn wooden floors were stained from spilled barbecue. If we sat near the cooler, we couldn't hear the conversation from the other side of the table. That corner of the Tavern was generally reserved for several old, nearly deaf black men who spent most of their afternoons shouting at each other over the noise while sipping beer.

Our teams always sat on the benches and tables outside, avoiding the combined racket of the old men and the cooler. The women visited inside, where they used worn hand fans to circulate the warm air. The fans were provided by the local funeral home. Kids ran in and out, slamming the screen doors, adding to the din and letting flies in. A large smoker at the back of the building used both oak and mesquite wood. When the barbecue was ready, the owners would step out the back door and bring it into the kitchen for slicing.

The Stars and Yellow Dogs enjoyed some very pleasant afternoons together at the Tavern. While we were sitting in the shade of the large trees, sipping beer and savoring the barbecue smells, Fat, the boldest of my teammates, asked me a personal question, the first I had heard from anyone: "White boy, Carl says you go to college. What's college like?"

The question caught me totally off-guard. I had wrongly assumed that everyone knew what college was like. I sat quietly for a few minutes while I thought of a response. No black students attended Tech at the time. I thought nothing of their absence because they weren't supposed to be there. I would have been shocked to see black students on campus. I don't recall even seeing black workers on campus. There were none in the dorms, cafeterias, or buildings, or on the ground crews.

I knew about all-black colleges, like Prairie View A&M, but I had never seen one. I could not even describe a school like that to them. I was at a loss for words, a circumstance that was unusual for me. I was ashamed and embarrassed about being a college student as I realized that for my teammates such an experience was as remote as the chance of their going to the moon.

In my stunned silence, I thought about my friends at Tech. Many knew the most superficial details of my summers at home, that I played semi-pro baseball, the name of the teams, and nothing else. It was just friendly conversation. Those who knew me well, some of my closest friends at

Tech, knew that this summer I was playing with an all-black team. Their initial reactions were of amazement and usually disbelief.

"Why are you doing that?" they'd ask.

The explanation got rather tiring, trying to make my white, rural friends understand why a reasonably sane white guy would do such a thing in a segregated world. A few of my fraternity brothers asked me if I'd become an "activist," meaning an active part of the Civil Rights Movement.

"No," I'd say. "We just like playing baseball together."

"What are black people really like? Weren't you afraid to be with them? Do you have a black girlfriend?" they'd ask.

In general, most of them at that time disapproved of what I was doing and were shocked that I did it. Consequently, I would hardly ever bring up the subject.

Instead of talking about the Tech students with the Stars, I decided to describe Lubbock, which none of my teammates had ever seen. I told them it was flat and treeless, surrounded by cotton fields, which caused some laughter. "Yes, we all know about cotton!" someone said. I smiled and blushed. We were trying to establish some common ground.

I told them how spread out the college grounds were, about the dust storms, the steam-heating systems for the buildings, and the number of students who attended the school. I explained that we had to study or we'd flunk out to make room for someone else who wanted a degree. They were very attentive.

"Are there any black students?" Bobby Lee Herron wanted to know.

"No, there aren't," I told him.

"Alfred Ray says you live in the biggest house in Jacksboro. Is that true?" Bobby asked.

"I don't think so, but it's a nice house, and I remember playing football and baseball with Alfred in our yard," I said.

"Growing up, did you have your own room?" Tommy asked.

"Yes, I did," I said. That information was received with several positive exclamations of "oh-umm!"

The Yellow Dogs were also listening to me. Then they started asking me questions, too. This was the first time members of an opposing team had taken an interest in my life. They wanted to know if I was married and how many cows I owned. I told them no, I was single, and recounted the number of cows on our ranch. They shook their heads in disbelief at the size of our herds.

After they had an opportunity to ask me questions, I felt very accepted by the Yellow Dogs, who seemed to be much more interested in my cows and horses than in my college life. College was totally beyond their comprehension. They had no hope of ever attending a university, but they understood farm animals and gardens. They were pleasant men, and I enjoyed their fellowship.

I learned to talk to them about everyday things, like what I had gathered from my mother's garden the day before.

"White people have gardens?" asked Fat, shaking his head in disbelief. Both teams were shocked. They thought that having a garden meant a family couldn't afford to buy food at the store. I tried to explain.

"Food tastes better when my mother grows it at home. She and I enjoy spending time in the garden," I told them.

Fat's gardening question and my answer began one of our longest and most animated conversations. Everyone had an opinion of what to grow in a garden and how to grow it. I wondered at how a simple conversation about gardening could bring two races together, but we all knew about it and wanted to share our information. After our gardening discussion, I asked them what they did for a living, how many kids they had, and where they went to church. I enjoyed listening to their answers.

While we visited at the Tavern, we also talked about subjects that ranged from Mr. Sedberry's love for the Negro Leagues to Fat's love for women. Fat always surveyed the groups of ladies sitting inside. I once asked him which one he thought was the prettiest. He pointed to a woman, and I told him, "Fat, that woman has a huge butt!"

"Why, white boy, women with little butts are not sexy!" he said.

These conversations may not appear to be intellectually and culturally significant, but we were establishing new territory for ourselves and our generation. Our postgame, presupper discussions did not involve solving the world's problems, or even those in Graham or Haskell. They were simple, pleasant visits. No one cared to prove he was smarter than another. We simply enjoyed each other's company.

When the Yellow Dogs would travel to play us, we always played them in Graham, not Wichita Falls, so that we could host them at Sedberry's Café. Mr. Sedberry challenged himself to provide the Yellow Dogs food that was equal to the Tavern's. He did his best by closing his café on Lincoln Street to everyone except the Yellow Dogs and their families and cooking barbecue for them.

To wash down the café's barbecue, our team would bring brands of beer I'd never seen or heard of. I'd ask, "Where in the world did you find this?"

"Why, at our liquor store, white boy!" they'd laugh. "And we bet it costs less than white folks' beer!"

I'd laugh, take a big swallow, and say, "Well, it just goes

to show you how dumb white folks are because this stuff sure is good." They would always laugh when I said that. Those meals are some of my favorite memories of my two seasons with the Stars. I thought about my conversations with the Stars, especially about how my college was segregated, and I told my parents about them, but they had no comment. I began to feel sorry for my teammates' plight. They would not have the education I would. Maybe *sorry* isn't the right word. I guess I was becoming aware of the opportunities that I had always taken for granted, and that realization made a lasting impression on me.

As I neared the end of my first season with the Stars, I began to anticipate road trips and understand the complexities of interacting with other teams, especially white ones. The Windthorst Trojans were a very competitive semi-pro team of German immigrant dairy farmers whose home field was behind the Catholic church, just below a hill. The only white team we knew who enjoyed baseball as much as we did, the Trojans were kinder to us than other white teams. Perhaps Windthorst's status as an immigrant community made its members more sympathetic to outsiders, though some of the Stars told me their white umpires could be unfair. The Trojans and Stars respected each other, and there was no mouthing between us. We played hard against each other.

Mr. Sedberry reported that their dugout had no water cooler, just kegs of beer. During our pregame meeting, he reminded us, "We need to get on this team early and hard because they become tough in the late innings." I never saw them act drunk, but by the later innings, I was sure a few of their players had consumed enough beer to see double.

"Don't you think their drinking might impair their playing?" I asked Mr. Sedberry.

"White boy, the more they drink, the better they play," he laughed.

"They could drink beer and still hit that ball. They couldn't hit home runs, but they hit everything that came across the plate," Rabbit later told me.

The game had started at 3:00 in the afternoon, but during the third inning, the Windthorst team called an unusual timeout, and several of their best players began to walk off the field.

"We have to go milk. We'll be back," they said to Mr. Sedberry as they waved good-bye to him. He nodded.

"What?" I asked him. "You're going to let them leave the game and return later?"

"We have to allow substitutions in the game so those players can go home and milk their cows. They milk their cows three times a day, game or no game," he said.

I had never seen anything like it. Several of their best players simply left the game and returned later. After they were done milking, Mr. Sedberry allowed them to return to their positions on the field to finish the game. Under the regular rules of baseball, once a player, like a pitcher, is pulled from a game, he may not pitch for the remainder of the game. A position player can move to a different position on the field but may not leave and return to his starting position. Temporary substitutions are not allowed.

As the players left the field and the substitutes started warming up, I asked Mr. Sedberry what we were supposed to do.

"Oh, Mr. Craft, we'll keep playing. They got plenty of players to use as substitutes. We have to let a few of them go milk, though. It's only fair to let those players return to the field. We can wait, but those cows can't," he said.

He was right. Despite the kegs in the Windthorst dugouts and the substitute players, we lost that game.

A few weeks later, Mr. Sedberry and my teammates wanted a Fourth of July game, but we couldn't find anyone to play us. So, he called the manager of the Windthorst team, and they agreed to a game. He told Mr. Sedberry they'd be happy to come to Graham if we'd provide the barbecue and beer for their families. Mr. Sedberry said he'd be happy to provide the food by hauling the smoker to the ballpark, but he couldn't provide the beer.

"In fact," Mr. Sedberry went on, "there's probably not enough beer in Young County for all of your ballplayers and fans!"

The town of Windthorst enjoyed celebrating America's independence. The patriotic town prided itself on support-ing the armed forces. During World War II fifty-two young men from Windthorst enlisted. The military took one glance at all the German names and sent them to fight in the South Pacific instead of Europe. The young men vowed that, if they lived, they would return to their hometown and build a grotto at the foot of the hill where St. Mary's Catholic Church stands. Each one, including Schroeders, Ostermanns, Schlabs, Weinzaphels, and Veitenhimers, returned and built the natural rock grotto. Square-cut sandstone lines the re-cessed memorial, with a statue of the Virgin Mary at its cen-ter. Near her is a plaque that describes the town's involvement in the war and lists the soldiers' names.

Those German names did not roll easily off Mr. Sed-berry's West Texas tongue as he read us their lineup card. We won the game probably due to the fact that most of the Windthorst substitutes stayed home to milk the cows, but that seemed secondary to both teams that day. We ate, drank, and watched each other's kids play together in the late afternoon sun. At dark we turned off the stadium lights and put on a fireworks display for the children. Different men, black and white, shot off bottle rockets and roman candles. I think the adults might have enjoyed the fireworks more than the kids did.

Earlier in the day I had taken off the blouse that I wore under my jersey because it was quite warm. That evening I was wearing a single layer, my old white cotton jersey. A strong wind from the south caused some of the children's sparklers to sputter and fade, flashing on and off in the dark like drunken fireflies. I volunteered to help, and they all gathered around me as I turned my back to the wind and began to light their sparklers again. One small black child's sparkler burst into unexpectedly bright sparks. Startled, he thrust it away from himself and into my jersey. I ran screaming around the infield, my shirt aflame, while the children chased me. They thought it was part of the grand celebration. They laughed and clapped for me when I finally stopped running to drop and roll out the flames. I still have the scars on my stomach from that performance.

The Stars talked about that Fourth of July for a long time. We talked about the game, the food, and the fun, but one detail of that day became special to me and Mr. Sedberry. We kept recalling the white kids and the black kids playing together while their parents socialized near them, fireworks lighting the air. This was unheard of in my time.

"Maybe, just maybe, times are beginning to change," Mr. Sedberry said to me. "Who would have thought that the Germans would be the ones?"

"Yes, that is ironic," I agreed.

His statement did not interest the rest of the Stars. I don't think they thought about life as deeply as Mr. Sedberry did. Our common interest, baseball, attracted us to one another, making us want to spend time together. Once we did, we discovered that we were really not all that much different. As we watched the fireworks, we were both concerned with equality and with the treatment of our families and friends in a segregated society. We thought the color of our skins shouldn't determine our lives, especially in the light of our mutual celebration of independence.

For the last game of my first season with the Stars, we faced our favorite rivals and buddies from Haskell, the Yellow Dogs, at home in Graham. We played them on a Sunday afternoon, the last weekend in August. The victory was bittersweet, capping a 31–1 season, because I knew a very special summer in my life had come to an end. After the game, we socialized at Sedberry's Café with our usual barbecue and beer.

We talked about what an exceptional year we had shared as a team. No one could remember winning thirty-one games in one season. We never kept individual statistics, but I knew my win-loss record was 16–1. I never mentioned this to them, believing that the team's record was more important than my own.

After our first season, I realized each player on the team was talented, but we lacked depth. If two or three key players were missing from our lineup, we could not win against a good ball club. To be a great team, we needed more pitchers and a bench. I was happy, though, to have been a part of the 1959 season.

I told my friends and teammates good-bye that day

because I would be leaving soon to return to Texas Tech and I needed to pack for school. Each one of them asked if I would play again next summer because they needed me to sustain a great team. I said yes, and some of us shook hands. I hugged my closest friends, Fat, Mr. Sedberry, Rabbit, and Fisher. We told each other how much we enjoyed our first season together and our friendships and how much we looked forward to next summer. I promised I'd be back, and I kept my promise.

SEVEN
Second Season

I RETURNED TO TEXAS TECH IN THE FALL of 1959 for my final year in college. Although my college days were collectively the happiest days of my young life, I missed baseball and the Stars. I knew I had shared something special with the Stars, which no white boy had ever experienced, and I wondered if my teammates felt the same way. I realized that they probably did not because while I had become a part of their world, their lives had changed very little. I looked forward to the next summer, 1960, when I could play for the Stars again.

Without baseball, there was a hole in my life. I had no Tech athletic scholarship, which made the hole feel even deeper. I decided the best way to survive missing baseball and the Stars was to keep myself busy with other physical activities. In the fall and early winter, I stayed in shape by juggling participation in the livestock judging team and in my fraternity's intramural football team. At times I marveled at how both activities involved handling and controlling pure animal strength, muscle, and instinct.

Livestock judging is a very competitive sport, and our team, coached by Dr. Stanley Anderson, won first place at Denver's Western Livestock Show and at the Fort Worth Fat Stock Show. Professor Anderson, a native of Iowa, was a square-jawed, dark-haired gentleman who wore dark-rimmed "Buddy Holly" glasses. He was a good teacher, very serious about teaching us to judge. Both he and Professor Pat Mowery, an elderly professor whose specialty was judging sheep, led us to the championships in Denver and at the Fort Worth Fat Stock Show, the Super Bowls of collegiate livestock judging.

When I wasn't working with the judging team, I played wide receiver and defensive halfback for my fraternity's football team, the Lions. On the practice fields southwest of Jones Stadium, we sprinted around in our purple and gold Sigma Alpha Epsilon uniforms, winning the college intramural championship with a record of 10–1. Jerry Pearson was our quarterback, and he and I were voted All-College intramural athletes for the fourth year in a row. I was glad to have been such an active member of Tech's intramural community that fall and looked forward to some much-needed rest in Jacksboro during the holidays.

Mr. Sedberry and I spoke on the phone during my Christmas break. In those conversations, I agreed to help him keep the Stars going, despite the difficulty he often faced filling his roster, scheduling games, and traveling to away games. We also talked about his work, my school, and our teammates. He encouraged me to make good grades, and I told him I was studying as often as possible.

Over the holidays, Mr. Sedberry also sent me a Christmas card. I showed it to my folks. It meant so much to me that I still have it. The front of the card depicts a black family gathered around a roaring fire, a lavishly decorated Christmas tree beside them. The well-dressed, handsome parents hand presents to their beautiful, beaming children. A set of grandparents watch the festive occasion from a comfortable couch in the corner. The card includes the following message: "Love, Carl, Mary, Dorene, and D.C."

My father gently turned it over and said, "Golly, if it weren't for the fact that they are all black, it looks just like any other family at Christmas!"

"Well, why wouldn't it look like this?" I asked him.

"I guess I never thought about blacks celebrating Christmas just like we do. Have you ever seen a card like this?" he wanted to know. I admitted that I had not. "I wonder where they found it." We both looked at the card as if it had arrived from outer space. I suddenly realized how little I really knew about the other race I claimed as my teammates and friends. I was not alone in my ignorance.

I remember that as a child I had been bewildered by separate rest rooms and drinking fountains for blacks and whites. During a trip to Fort Worth, I couldn't comprehend why I wasn't allowed to drink from a fountain in Woolworth's department store. My mother grabbed my arm and exclaimed, "Jerry, you can't drink from that water! See the sign? It says 'colored.'"

"Mom, the water looks clear to me," I said.

"Jerry, white people have their own toilets and water," she said.

"Why?" I asked.

"Because," was all she said.

I also recall segregation in Jacksboro when I was a child, but as a small town we had a few opportunities to get to know each other better than people living in the larger cities did. I got my hair cut at Mack Brown's Barber Shop on the south side of Jacksboro's town square on Saturdays. I rode my bike there and left it at the red, white, and blue barber pole that spiraled outside by the parking meter. The barbershop filled me with apprehension and awe. It was narrow and long, running all the way back to the next street to the south and lined with half a dozen chairs. Dark wood surrounded me, and the place reeked of cheap hair tonic, aftershave lotion, shoe polish, and cigars.

The first person who always greeted me in the shop was Cecil Williams, the black man whom customers called "the shoe-shine boy." My father, like the other men in town who could afford it, dropped off his shoes and boots for Cecil to shine. Cecil was a happy, pleasant man who'd laugh and say, "Come in here, little J. D.!"

After dropping off their shoes, my father and his friends would have their hair cut and then drift toward the back room of the barbershop for a shot of Mack's bootleg bourbon. This same group of men also loved to take their hound dogs out at night to track game and tree raccoons. They included Cecil in their hunting trips. He cooked for them and hauled their equipment. My father was very fond of Cecil and cried when he died. My father's grief frightened and confused me because I had never seen him cry before that day. I am at a loss to explain this contradiction in my father, who truly seemed to care for this black man. Perhaps it was my father's opinion that "Cecil knew his place" that allowed him to develop a fondness for a particular black man.

* * *

When I returned to Tech in the spring of 1960, two of my fraternity brothers, Charlie Stenholm and Jerry Pearson, and I were voted All-College in softball. Pearson and I held that honor four straight years. I also received the Hutton Memorial Trophy for outstanding senior athlete. Intramural sports had helped me mature by teaching me teamwork and discipline, and I was ready for real life, including graduation.

My sister, Linda, and I graduated on the same day, she from Louisiana State University with a degree in psychology and I from Tech with a degree in Animal Husbandry and a minor in Journalism. Linda had acquired a rather phony southern accent during her time at LSU, which the family found unbearable. Our slow West Texas drawls stalled next to her deep South twang. She grew impatient with us and sounded very out-of-place, both in speech and topic. My father was beginning to regret having sent her away to college.

One night after supper, she was lamenting the lack of eligible and attractive bachelors in Jacksboro. My father immediately went for her jugular with, "Why don't you go with your brother to a Stars game? He can introduce you to his black teammates. I'm sure they talk just like you do!"

The bell rang, and the two met in the middle of the kitchen for the night's main event. I felt like hiding under the table. My mother grew very pale and quiet. As Mr. Sedberry would say, "Whoo-boy!"

During these heated confrontations, neither Linda nor my father would back down or say they were wrong or sorry. They continued to argue until my mother would stop them. Then they would "sull up," silently moping around the house, until they were ready to talk to each other again, which was usually the next day. The next time they spoke to one another, they acted as if nothing had ever happened. They reminded me of stubborn cows or bulls that would "sull up" when we would try to load them into a trailer. They would stand still, heads down, refusing to move.

Despite embarrassing my family during the 1959 season, I had pledged to my Stars teammates that I would return the following summer. I was a man of my word, and I looked forward to another season with my friends. I was really expecting a repeat of the same magical year we had in 1959, but that didn't happen.

By 1960 the Civil Rights Movement was gaining momentum, and my community was beginning to sense the change. Every night on television my family and I watched angry blacks and whites protesting and marching for their rights. When I discussed integration with my white friends, I told them that I played with an all-black baseball team during the previous summer and found my teammates to be essentially the same as white people. My black teammates loved their wives and kids and worked hard to make a living. I also added that during the times I had spent with them, they seemed happier than my white friends. None of my teammates or their friends had the opportunity to earn a college education, but they knew integration was coming, and their lives might improve. However, they did not want integration forced upon them. They, like their white neighbors, feared the unknown.

Sometimes a bigot in my peer group questioned my desire to play on a black baseball team, but my friends who had been to college or were college graduates were more tolerant. My college friends and I were not afraid of integration the way the Stars were. We were young, and our educations provided us the ability to examine our thoughts and belief systems. We could accept change more easily because we had been through a four-year educational process that included learning to ask difficult questions and make tough, complicated decisions about our lives.

By the time the Stars and I played our first game in May of 1960, our country had witnessed several impressive events. In February four black students from North Carolina Agricultural and Technical College demanded lunch at Woolworth's in Greensboro and were refused service, starting other nonviolent racial protests in the South. By August the same four students were finally served their lunches. In March the military announced that 3,500 American troops were being sent to Vietnam, and the U.S. Senate passed the Civil Rights Bill on April 21. These events took place miles away from Jacksboro, but I knew they were important. The events of 1960, including my second season with the Stars, have become increasingly significant to me over the years. Back then, though, I was simply looking forward to playing baseball again with my friends.

Before the start of the first Stars game of the 1960 season, I learned that tragedy had struck our team the same day I had returned to Tech for the fall semester. No one contacted me in Lubbock with the news. They didn't know how to find me, and they wouldn't have called my parents. If I had known what happened, I would have immediately returned to them because I was their teammate and they were my friends. We had made much progress building our friendships while we were playing ball and traveling together, but I was really not a part of their lives once I left for school. After the baseball season, they resumed their lives, and I mine. Except for Mr. Sedberry and his Christmas card, they didn't think about me until spring when the promise of another baseball season was in the air. Then my teammates thought, "I wonder where our white boy is?"

Mr. Sedberry took me aside when I first arrived at the field. He told me what had happened after I left the party at his café following the final game of the 1959 season. The Stars ran out of beer, so Mr. Sedberry and four of my teammates, Alfred Ray, Tommy Jones, Emmitt Johnson, and Hubert "Bo" Beasley, left Sedberry's Café and drove to Possum Kingdom Lake to buy more. They were headed toward a little place called Bungalow, just across the county line. Alfred was sitting in the front passenger seat.

On the way to the lake they ran off old Bunger Road and hit a large post oak tree. Alfred was thrown through the windshield. Mr. Sedberry watched him fly over his head and out of the car. Alfred's back was broken. He was paralyzed and died in Graham Hospital a few days later. He was buried in the Oakwood Cemetery in Jacksboro.

I subscribed to our hometown newspapers while I was away at Tech so that I could read about the events in Jacksboro. There weren't many, but I always read the obituaries. I missed news of Alfred's death because back then black people weren't allowed to place obituaries in the white papers. If I had known, I would have attended Alfred Ray's funeral, just as years later I attended Bobby Herron's and Mr. Sedberry's.

Mr. Sedberry gently patted me on the back and told me that Emmitt would take Alfred's place as catcher. I grasped his hand and told him I was very sorry about Alfred. My teammates had gathered around me as Mr. Sedberry told the story, and my sincere sorrow at Alfred's passing touched them. I'm sure as baseball players they realized the special bond that forms between a pitcher and a catcher. While I was disappointed no one had called me about Alfred, I recognized the fact that I was their friend and teammate, but I was not a member of their everyday world.

With our starting catcher gone, the Stars were not the same. I recall fewer games from our second season than I do from our first. The first season was bright with new experiences for me, but the second is dimmer because I knew we weren't as good. I was often frustrated with our quality of play during 1960, and I think my mind simply chooses to linger on the pleasanter year of 1959. Like innings, some memories are longer and more distinct than others.

I knew our time was short and our light was fading, but we had a large, happy crowd on that first Sunday afternoon at Spudder Park in late May of 1960. Mr. Sedberry had prepared well for the opener and had "done things up brown," an old southern term for arranging a first-class show. (The term sounds racial, so it's not used very often anymore.) The fans were amazed to see us resplendent in brand-new uniforms. We had been measured for them at the Bobby Evans and Paul Brotherton Sporting Goods Store in Wichita Falls and picked them up when Mr. Sedberry called to tell us they were ready. We had also been individually fitted for our cap size. Even our blue stockings were new. I switched my white cotton pitcher's sweatshirt to a blue-sleeved one to match everyone else. I was reluctant, though, because I thought the white sleeves looked better and hid the baseball better.

Our uniforms were light gray with navy blue pinstripes and navy blue cording around the neck and down the front, where five blue buttons shone brightly in the sun. The word "Stars" in navy blue ran across the chest. Mine had the number 6 on the left sleeve. My back read "Faith Cleaners" from Wichita Falls, its motto "The City That Faith Built." The pants were short knickers style with a four-button fly and matching navy blue stockings. No ballplayers were ever prouder of their uniforms than my teammates and I were on that day. We were each responsible for the care and cleaning of our own uniforms, something we did eagerly.

Mr. Sedberry found a recording of the national anthem to open the game. I stood by my teammates and proudly listened to the music of our country. We were all citizens of the United States. We were truly united as we listened to the same anthem, watched the same flag, and wore matching uniforms for the first time. Most teams and fans would take this scene for granted at the start of every game, but for us it was a special day. I took my cap off and placed it over my heart while the music played. All of my teammates did the same. They seemed very happy to be playing baseball again, but I was still recovering from the shock and grief of not having Alfred with us that day. I tried to put on a brave smile for the crowd, who seemed impressed that their Stars now had uniforms.

Mr. Sedberry had solicited local businesses in Graham and Wichita Falls to donate a uniform apiece with the business's name on the back. He claimed he had no trouble with the donations because we had made quite a name for ourselves among the black community during the summer of 1959. Our winning record made the east side's businesses want to be associated with us, and they knew the fans would see their names on our backs everywhere we went. As businessmen, they recognized the need to advertise.

This was a new phenomenon in Wichita Falls, whose black population and businesses were slowly being integrated. In 1960 the federal government mandated that Booker T. Washington High School be closed and the east side's students be bused to the city's white schools. Two new schools, Hershi and Rider, were built. Then, the inevitable happened.

With the relocation of their children, many of the black parents moved from the east side of town to the west side of town. Black businesses that had once had a monopoly were losing customers and money.

I can remember several times after games in 1959 my teammates and I would walk to a black restaurant or bar. By 1960, our choices of eating establishments within walking distance of Spudder Park had become somewhat limited. Businesses had closed and were boarded up. Pride had left with the high school students.

"Mr. Craft," Mr. Sedberry said as he glanced at the empty storefronts, "my race is beginning to lose its identity."

"I understand what you mean," I said, and I told him that in rural Texas small schools were often forced to consolidate with a larger town's school system. The rural children were then bused to town to attend school. The small towns withered and died when the young people left.

Mr. Sedberry, however, seemed much more optimistic for the opening game. After the anthem, a new loudspeaker system blared "Sweet Georgia Brown," and my teammates laughed and showed off during our warm-ups. They tossed baseballs from behind their backs, rolled them down their arms to their hands, and caught them with their caps, all the while doing neat little dance steps, similar to line dancing. They would sometimes stand along the infield foul line and dance together to the music. Fat led the choreography, but Puddin and Bo could boogie, too.

Mr. Sedberry was pleased with himself and the festive arrangements. He laughed a lot and said, "Everything is fine in the summertime!" He had grieved for Alfred months ago, and now the start of a new baseball season made him extremely cheerful.

I appreciated his enthusiasm, but my mood darkened

when I learned whom Mr. Sedberry had chosen for us to face on opening day. A brand-new semi-pro team from Bowie, Texas, had just arrived at the field. The Jackrabbits were an all-white team because everyone in Bowie was white, and their dislike of blacks was very well known. My anxiety increased when our pregame celebration ended and the game began.

I was on the mound, and Emmitt Johnson was now my catcher, replacing Alfred as best he could. The Jackrabbits were not a good ball club, and we were beating them badly. The Stars, who had shared a few beers with their fans in the stands before the game, started berating the other team. My teammates were calling out things like, "Do you *boys* play Little League on Saturdays?" I had never seen the Stars behave this way in front of a white team before. The new uniforms, the Opening Day festivities, and the large lead caused them to act boldly, and their behavior was probably a mistake. The white players were seething. They weren't taking the ribbing or the humiliation well from my teammates. I found it amusing, but Mr. Sedberry said nothing. He was intent on winning the game.

Around the bottom of the eighth inning, Bobby Herron showed up. He had been working late and refused to wear a new Stars uniform. He had on his old Monarchs duds instead. My teammates understood and didn't have a problem with his wearing it, though I think Mr. Sedberry would have preferred we all matched.

Bobby eyed the score and the new opposition and said, "Where are these white peckerwoods from?"

"Bowie," Fat said.

If a black person could turn white, Bobby came close to it.

With a pale, scared glance at Mr. Sedberry, he said, "Carl, have you arranged for us to play them at their home field next week?"

"Yes, we play them in Bowie next Sunday afternoon," he replied. "Why do you want to know?"

"Boys, do you know what they'll do to us in Bowie?" Bobby asked us. Bobby then recounted several vivid atrocities that happened to blacks who foolishly traveled through Bowie. I had heard the stories, too, and I guess some may have been true. We heard that whites in Bowie felt blacks weren't worth shooting. Hanging and burning were preferred. Strangely, I was hearing these stories for the first time from my teammates' perspective. I, however, remained optimistic that times had changed.

"I am afraid to go to Bowie, too," Rabbit said. "I remember the first time I went from Wichita to Dallas. I went through Bowie, and they had a black man on the road hung by his neck."

"Hey, guys," I said. "That happened a long time ago. There's nothing to worry about now."

"Oh yeah, white boy? Why does the concrete bridge at the west edge of Bowie still have the words 'Nigger, don't let the sun set on your back in Bowie' painted on it?" he asked me. A few of my teammates verified they had recently seen it. So had I.

They were terrified. When we took the field again, I'd never seen us make so many errors. If we hadn't already built up such a sizable lead, I'm sure we would have lost that game. We finally got out of the inning, but there was no joy in Mudville. Our team no longer taunted the Jackrabbits, worried about how they might retaliate in Bowie, but Mr.

Sedberry thought the right thing to do would be to keep his agreement to play there. We reluctantly told him we'd meet next Sunday in Bowie.

To my surprise, the Stars drove in from Wichita Falls for the game in Bowie, and I came by myself from Jacksboro. Every single one of the Stars came ready to play, even though they were scared to death. No chatter or horseplay occurred before the game. Our fans must have been smarter than we were because not one black person sat in the bleachers that day. Without our usual raucous fan support, the mood on the field was somber.

As we went through our warm-ups, I glanced from the mound into the crowd. I watched a very large Bowie fan wander down the front of the bleachers. He had a crew cut and was wearing coveralls and a white T-shirt, the front of it slightly splattered from the huge chew of tobacco in his jaw. He waved to some of his friends in the stands as he shuffled along with his thumbs resting on the inside of his overall straps. Then, with his back to the field, he visited with a couple on the first row. As he turned to face the field for the first time, he actually staggered back as if he had been hit with a two-by-four.

A look of disbelief spread over his beefy face, and, with a quivering finger, he pointed to the field. In a voice that could be heard over all of Montague County, he boomed, "My Gawd almighty. There's niggers in Bowie!"

My teammates ducked their heads and tried to disappear into the dugout. I gave them a pep talk and reminded them that what had happened was in the distant past. I even took it a step further and said, "You always tell me not to worry and that you'll take care of me. I pledge to take care of you today."

"Jerry, there's only one of you," Rabbit reminded me, glancing quickly at the large, all-white crowd.

I looked around and feared the worst. Although the entire Bowie police force and the Montague County Sheriff's department were present, I did not want to take my chances on their protecting me. Our adrenaline must have been at an all-time high because Rabbit and Bobby hit their first two pitches so far over the fence no one ever found the balls. The Bowie crowd's enthusiasm immediately deflated, their fans' and the team's egos barely hovering over the field like old helium balloons.

A few innings later, I gave up back-to-back home runs, the only game in which I ever did that. However, I overcame that setback to pitch well that day, and we whipped them badly. When the last out was called, the Stars jumped in their cars and got the hell out of Dodge. There was no tailgating after that game, and we never scheduled another game with the Jackrabbits.

The game in Bowie put our team under great psychological stress, and several of our regular players didn't attend the next few games. Our season was starting to suffer, and we were losing games. We were also in danger of not having enough players to field a team for the popular Juneteenth tournament, which surprised me because my teammates really looked forward to that tournament and celebration, especially when they were given time off from work to play. At that time employers recognized the importance of Juneteenth and granted their black employees time off from work.

With the extra time off, we participated in one weekend tournament a year, the annual Juneteenth Tournament in Ranger, Texas. Juneteenth commemorates June 19, 1865, the date that U.S. General Gordon Granger read the Emancipation Proclamation in Galveston. President Lincoln had issued the proclamation in Washington, D.C., on September

22, 1862, and it went into effect on January 1, 1865, for most of the country. However, several states, including Texas, were still in rebellion and therefore did not abide by the proclamation until U.S. forces resumed control over them. News of the proclamation was reported in Texas newspapers in the fall of 1862, but until General Granger and his occupying forces landed on Texas soil in 1865, the proclamation was not in effect. Juneteenth was a huge celebration in Texas in the late 1950s and early 1960s, and the Stars enjoyed the holiday by playing in the Ranger tournament.

The first year I played in the tournament, 1959, we won the championship game against a black team from Anna, a small Collin County town northeast of Dallas. Encouraged by our strong performance, Mr. Sedberry mailed our entrance fee early in our second season, assuming we'd have the same strong team. He could not have anticipated that our team would be weaker in 1960. However, we had paid for the tournament, and he insisted that we appear. We couldn't let our fans down.

The fans were, in fact, the best part of the tournament. All of the Stars fans plus fans of teams from all over Texas traveled to those games. Fat told me he had never seen so many black people in a white town at one time. In fact, Fat began planning for the tournament early. He decided not to invite one of his many lady friends as he had done in 1959 because he had observed plenty of women traveling from all over Texas to see the black teams. He was like a kid in a candy store, and he knew that for the second tournament he'd have something new for his sweet tooth.

We received the brackets a few weeks before the games, but I don't have any idea how they were organized. I noticed that teams local to Ranger played on Friday night to give teams like us more time to travel. It didn't really matter who we played because we were facing black teams we'd never played before. We knew nothing about them, which created an interesting series of games.

In 1960 Mr. Sedberry began scouting new players because he wanted to win the tournament. He discovered that the talented black players in the area already played for other teams. When I heard his unsuccessful scouting report, I had an idea. I was worried Mr. Sedberry might not appreciate my input, but I didn't want to play for a losing team, especially one that had enjoyed tremendous success during the previous season. I decided to talk to him while we were packing our equipment after a particularly brutal loss to Fort Wolters.

"I have a couple of friends in Jacksboro who might like to play for the Stars. Of course, they're both white," I said.

He stopped what he was doing and looked me in the eye. Finally he said, "Let me talk to the team about your proposal." I knew that he might be open to the idea because he had invited me to join the Stars. I hoped that my teammates would be willing to play with my white friends as well.

Mr. Sedberry motioned for the Stars to stop loading their cars and join us. Then he turned to the team and said, "Jerry wants to bring a couple of his white friends along to play next time. What do you think of that?"

"If Jerry recommends them and they're anything like him, let them play," Rabbit said. Everyone nodded, and the mood brightened as they knew wins were more fun than losses. The Stars wouldn't have cared if my friends were purple if they could play baseball. I promised to talk to Monroe Henderson and Tony Clark as soon as possible so that the Stars could add much-needed depth to the team.

Later that week I spoke to Monroe and Tony. They already

knew about my playing with a black team, but they had not considered playing with them until I extended the invitation and told them the Stars were happy to have them.

Monroe and Tony loved playing baseball and readily agreed to play for the Stars, but they wouldn't be able to join us until the championship game on Sunday at the Juneteenth Tournament. Monroe was especially eager to come to the tournament. He enjoyed every baseball club he joined. He later told me it didn't make any difference to him that the Stars were a black team, but he probably wouldn't have joined them on his own. I had to ask him first. He was glad I did it because he would not have met the Stars, their fans, and their family members otherwise. He loved playing baseball, and the days of having our pick of which semi-pro club we wanted to play with were rapidly fading as we grew older.

Monroe remembers his reason for joining the Stars was competition, pure competition. He was always trying to make himself a better baseball player. He would read books about baseball, getting tips on how to hit. When he was a kid, he built his own sliding pit in the sand near his family's horse barn and ordered spikes from Montgomery Ward, which cost about a dollar. He tacked them on the bottom of his shoes and practiced sliding for hours. He thought that his makeshift spikes would improve his ability to play baseball.

When the Stars finally arrived late Friday evening in Ranger, we watched the end of the games the local teams were playing so we could start our warm-ups as soon as they were finished. We never had enough fields for everyone to play during the day, so we played all night Friday and into Saturday. I had learned about the all-night games our first year in Ranger, making a fool out of myself in the process.

In 1959 when I had asked what motel we'd use in Ranger, my teammates laughed at me. Bobby said, "White boy, there's no place we can all stay in Ranger." I hadn't thought of that and looked sheepishly at my bag of clean underwear, socks, jersey, and toiletries. My teammates graciously overlooked my extra clothes, and their good nature soon set me at ease again.

I would have enjoyed staying in a motel so that I could shower and change, but my desire to be a true member of the team outweighed my desire to smell good. When Bobby added, "We sleep in our cars, but we don't expect you to do that," I told them I'd sleep in my car, too. They stared at me in disbelief for a moment. Then they looked at each other and grinned. I undressed to my T-shirt and shorts, wadded up my uniform for a pillow, and stuck my feet out of the passenger window so that I could sleep in my backseat.

Mr. Sedberry gently approached the car and said, "Mr. Craft, you don't have to do this."

"Yes, I do," I said.

A few minutes later, Rabbit brought me a spare pillow and some mosquito spray. He hesitated, then added, "Good night. You're a good man."

That night I was uncomfortable and hot. I didn't get a lot of sleep. Neither did they, but I gained a new respect among my teammates and a few stiff muscles.

Later that next morning, I gathered up some money and drove to Ranger to buy us hamburgers and chips. We already had soda and beer iced down, but I bought the food because Ranger and its restaurants were segregated.

By the second tournament, I was prepared to camp. I'd packed plenty of pillows, blankets, and mosquito spray. I was more comfortable, but we didn't sleep much because we were having such a good time. Parties would start late at night and continue until the next day. We had little time to get any rest.

I pitched Friday night's game against Hamlin, which we won. We partied all night Friday and into Saturday morning, drinking and visiting with one another and the other teams and spectators in the stands. A team that lost early and was out of the tournament stayed for the fun. Everyone camped at the tournament because they couldn't go into Ranger. The crowded conditions made the tournament a little rowdy at times, but most of us enjoyed meeting new people and talking to them.

We were a bit dirty and smelly by game time on Saturday. Fat pitched, and we won, qualifying us for the Sunday afternoon championship game against San Augustine, a small town in far east Texas next to the Louisiana border. Monroe and Tony arrived in time for the game, and Monroe started at third base. Tony played right field, and I pitched, winning 5–3. Monroe remembers that he and Tony wore Stars uniforms for the games. Tony, Monroe, and I were the only white players, and the only white spectator for the entire tournament was Tony's wife, Linda, who sat in the stands for the championship game.

I never understood why white people didn't watch the tournament. The tremendous level of play and the excitement of tournament baseball would have made any sports fan happy, black or white. The whites in Ranger must have noticed the large number of blacks coming through town to attend the tournament. The locals may have felt unsafe there, or it may not have been acceptable for them to attend.

When Monroe and Tony joined us for the championship game, we shifted Vernon "Puddin" Higgins from third to second so that Monroe could play third base. Monroe was the best ballplayer of my era from Jacksboro. I wasn't even in his league. He was a superior infielder with a strong throwing arm. He could play shortstop or third base with equal ease and was devastating at the plate. He usually got at least two hits a game, often a home run.

Tony, on the other hand, was not a great athlete, but he was a good outfielder and could play second base for us in a pinch. He was a couple of years younger than Monroe and was simply pleased to be offered the chance to play baseball with us. He had loved the game since he was a kid, and even though he was a mediocre player, he knew the game well and played it at every opportunity.

The Stars had become very comfortable playing with me, but with two more white players on the team, I believe my teammates were a little uneasy about unleashing their usual verbal assaults. I noticed that my black teammates were making a conscious effort not to be overly aggressive or to say anything offensive. They were all kinder and more considerate with three white guys around. Even the all-black opposition stopped the usual barrage of racial slurs. A fair amount of bench-jockeying continued—it wouldn't be baseball without it—but the banter never touched on color, ancestry, or any other sensitive area.

Monroe does not remember any resentment from the Stars when he and Tony joined the team for the tournament. He thinks if they felt any, they disguised it. Monroe really didn't expect any trouble, and he doesn't remember any. The Stars were happy to have their help. If it meant the team could win the tournament, then the experience would be fun.

He later told me he was just there to play ball. He didn't care what the people said. He had played in hostile environments, but the tournament wasn't one of them. When he played for Texas Tech against Sam Houston State in Huntsville, Texas, he played third base. Third base was really close to the sidelines with chicken wire separating the fans from the players. The college students from Sam Houston would climb on the chicken wire and yell at him. Nothing like that ever happened when he played for the Stars.

Linda sat happily among the black fans in the stands, and they went out of their way to make her feel welcome. Tony told her years later that the game amounted to an awakening for him. For the first time in his life, he saw people with their masks at least partly down. In their eyes he found pride and a wide range of emotions lacking in his white friends. His new teammates were exuberant, fully dimensional human beings who had many of the same needs, dreams, and desires he did. He told Linda he was ashamed that he had largely ignored his black neighbors before the tournament, and the game changed his life.

After the final game, Tony, Linda, Monroe, and I caravanned to a barbecue dinner at the all-white Ranger Country Club, which the teams had somehow rented. I don't know how they arranged it or what it cost, but we were all there. Ranger originated in the 1870s as a Texas Ranger campsite, but by 1919 it was an oil boom town. In 1960 Ranger was home to some very affluent families, a fine country club, and a nice golf course.

Tony later told me that as he stood in the crowd at the country club, he felt for the first time in his life some ill-defined sense of what it might be like to be a minority. Everyone was polite, but several times people looked startled when they saw him. They weren't expecting to see him there, though the fact that he was in a baseball uniform probably helped minimize the shock and explain his and Monroe's presence.

"I feel welcome, but I don't feel like I belong," he told me shortly before he, Linda, and Monroe left. "We're intruding on a very cherished and private time for a people upon whom we have already imposed enough."

"It's OK," I told him. "Please stay. You helped us win today, so you are a part of us."

"No, we're calling it an evening. I believe I've learned a lot in a few hours about a whole group of people I've lived beside all my life but have never known." They all thanked me as we said our good-byes. After Tony and his group left the party, I noticed that the crowd relaxed. They had seen me around before, and I no longer distracted them.

Before my teammates and I could eat and socialize, we needed a good shower. We were lucky enough to enjoy hot showers, soap, and clean towels at the country club. Showers were a wonderful luxury that teams today take for granted. That was our first shower as a team in nearly two years.

The large, open shower room had about ten shower heads. Both teams from the championship game had a real soaker, and we popped each other with towels and sang songs. I looked as naked as a lone daisy in a clover patch.

Looking around me, I proclaimed in a loud voice, "Well, guys, as a white man, I have to agree that what they say about a black man's anatomy is sure true!"

They all paused, and then someone glanced at me and said, "Well, what they say about a white man's lack of it is also true!" We roared with laughter during what was possibly the first integrated team shower.

We hated dressing in our sweaty uniforms after showering, but we had no extra clothes. As we emerged from the locker rooms, a wonderful smell surrounded our slightly stale one. Designated chefs had been at their trade all day, cooking barbecue. Slow cookers lined the room, full of chicken, brisket, and ribs for the nearly three hundred players, family, and friends who were enjoying full access to the country club.

The beer flowed so fast that by the third round it wasn't cold, but no one cared. The food was excellent. As we sat around the twenty-five tables or so, having a great time, out of the blue a fight erupted. Two women started it, and, ignorant white boy that I was, I had never seen women really fight. I had seen a couple of white girls slap each other, but these women were rolling over the tables, pulling out handfuls of hair, screaming, cussing, choking, and punching each other. Food and plates flew everywhere. Everyone around me immediately began betting on who would win. I had honestly never seen or heard anything like it.

There were cries of, "I'll take her! OK, I'll take her!" as the bettors threw down money on the tables.

About the time the women were winding down, a fight between two men broke out at the other end of the room. Part of the crowd from the women's fight rushed over to the men's fight and began betting there. As I sat and watched with my teammates, I said, "Guys, it's time for this white boy to go home." I was certain that the fights would eventually end, but I didn't know if they were going to get any worse.

Mr. Sedberry said, "Mr. Craft, we told you we would always take care of you, and we will."

"I know," I said. "You always have, but it's dark out there, and I'm afraid someone will think I'm black and beat the hell out of me!"

We all had a good laugh, and I told them I'd see them on Wednesday. When June 19 rolls around each year, I always think of the two wonderful weekends I spent celebrating Juneteenth.

EIGHT
Lessons from a Black Man

FTER THE EXCITEMENT OF THE JUNETEENTH tournament,
Mr. Sedberry wanted to keep us busy. He felt that
our season had taken a turn for the better, and he
intended to maintain our positive momentum. He
was thrilled when the Trojans invited us to play on the
Fourth of July at Windthorst. We had played them at Graham
on the Fourth of July during the previous season. That game
had been such a success that their team wanted to return
the favor. This year the Trojans included all of the families in
the festivities and provided the postgame fireworks. The
Windthorst team was just as gracious as they had been the
year before, and this time we ate German sausage instead of
barbecue as we watched the fireworks.

The Trojans were as tough as ever. We expected them to

be, and I was hoping the Stars had regained some of the confidence of the 1959 season by continuing our rivalry with the Trojans. This Fourth of July they had a new baseball field, a tremendous improvement from the pasture we had played on the year before. They also had a new catcher named Schribener who played at Texas A&M. He was a handsome man, well built, with a black flattop haircut. I believe he hated to lose as much as I did.

A large crowd, half black and half white, sat in the July sun, enjoying the game and each other. Although the Stars, Trojans, and their fans got along, they did not sit together. The stands appeared to be segregated because the white fans got to the game first, and they sat wherever they liked. That's where the rest of the white fans joined them. When the black fans arrived, they sat on the other side. Behind home plate a five-foot gap divided the blacks and the whites. I suppose that they could have chosen to sit closer together, but that just wasn't done back then. I don't think they were necessarily segregating themselves by race, just by the team they supported.

Of all the white teams we played against, we were most comfortable facing Windthorst. Nevertheless, they were a white team, and we were playing them on their home field in front of their white fans. As I've mentioned, the Stars toned down the insults with white teams, particularly on their home fields. There was still chatter, but seldom anything worse than one of the Stars calling out to me, "He can't hit what he can't see!"—meaning that I should use my fastball. It was a white man's world, and the Stars knew their place.

About an hour into the game, the Windthorst dairy farmers again began making their temporary substitutions. It was milking time. I was still amused by the fact that we allowed them to go milk their cows in the middle of a baseball game, but I wasn't a dairy farmer. I was a rancher, and ranchers don't milk. Certain times of the year are busier for us than others, but we don't have the daily commitment to milking that dairy farmers do. As I watched them leave for their farms, I was grateful I was a rancher.

Even without the dairy farmers participating, the game was a close one. In the top of the ninth, Wayne Fisher was on second and I was on first. Rabbit slammed a high, outside fastball, nearly out of right center. There was only one out, so Fisher and I hesitated until the ball banged off the top of the fence and back into the field of play before we started running. Fisher was a powerful left-handed first baseman, but his injured foot's awkward angle slowed him down as he rounded third and headed for home. I was not far behind him. Mr. Sedberry waved both of us in.

"Run, Fisher! Run!" I hollered behind him.

The Windthorst catcher Schribener had his mask off and was crouched on the third-base side of home plate, waiting for the throw, his huge left leg angled to protect the plate. Fisher made a beautiful hook slide with his right leg toward the front of the plate. Schribener caught the throw and dove for Fisher, but the tag was too late. Fisher caught the front of the plate with his good foot.

I heard the umpire call "Safe!" and signal as I slid head-first to the backside of the plate, my left hand extended. Schribener reacted quickly, lunging for me, but again tagging just a little too late.

"Safe! Safe! I'll be damned! They're both safe!" the umpire screamed.

Schribener didn't argue. We were all stunned about what had just happened. A crippled hitter and a pitcher had both scored on an extremely tough catcher in close plays at the plate. I've never seen that happen before or since. The crowd seemed equally stunned. Then both sides stood up and clapped. They hollered, slapped each other's backs, and exclaimed they'd never seen anything like it either. One of the unique things about the game of baseball is that average players can sometimes achieve greatness in the face of adversity, and average fans can appreciate a great play. At those times, both players and fans are color blind.

We all talked about the play a great deal as we celebrated the Fourth after the game, final score Stars 5, Trojans 4. We had played very good baseball in Windthorst, against a solid ball club. When all of our players were present, we could beat anyone in our league.

The town was incredibly supportive of the game, turning out to see us play and to eat with us afterward. As in Graham, we again enjoyed watching the children during the fireworks display. A couple of tables full of food were set up by the slow cookers, holding piles of German sausage. We passed down the line of tables, holding our paper plates, and the cooks would serve us the sausage.

After we filled our plates and found some beer, everyone sat in the bleachers and ate. Although the game was over, they still sat separately in the stands. The children cheered the fireworks display, watching as the adults set off bottle rockets, cherry bombs, sparklers, and roman candles.

Our spirits had been lifted during the Fourth of July holiday game in Windthorst, so Mr. Sedberry decided to schedule a rare doubleheader in distant Oklahoma City. He claimed he couldn't get anyone else to play that weekend and that the Braves wanted a doubleheader. If we were to travel all the way to Oklahoma, we might as well play two.

A 140-mile drive north of Wichita Falls did not appeal to our team, whose members were becoming increasingly reluctant to play games away from Wichita Falls or Graham because we had little depth on the bench. Our left-handed pitcher T. J. Hawkins couldn't hit or field, and he had less than perfect attendance at games. Right-handed pitcher Sam "Bam" Brown's attendance was even worse than T. J.'s hitting and fielding.

Without Sam and T. J. we had no bench. This situation wasn't unique to semi-pro baseball teams of our era. Substitute players who rode the bench more than they played soon found better things to do on Sunday afternoons. Without a bench and with the increasingly frequent absences of one or two of the top players, we started to lose more games than we won. We had never fully recovered from the death of catcher and co-captain Alfred Ray. He had been an excellent catcher and a tremendous leader. No one filled that void.

The loss of a catcher was truly problematic for our team. When Mr. Sedberry lamented his lack of players, he always reminded us, "It's hard to find a good catcher." He would again explain to everyone within earshot, "It's a dirty, dangerous, tiring position. Your knees give out because you're involved in every play, crouching behind home plate, and no one in the stands appreciates that. The fans see an outfielder make a diving catch, and they will applaud wildly, but a catcher might have to do that every fourth pitch, and no one notices, except when the ball gets past him."

Mr. Sedberry had replaced Alfred with Emmitt Johnson, our second baseman who did his best behind the plate, but he was not a gifted catcher. Emmitt and Rabbit were our new team co-captains. They were great leaders, but shifting our infield had created a domino effect of gaping holes in the lineup for Mr. Sedberry. Next he moved Hawkins to second, but he was as useless there as at the plate.

Monroe made the Oklahoma City trip, and we rode there

together in my car. Mo didn't care where we were playing. He simply enjoyed playing and was happy to help the Stars again after his enjoyable experience at the Ranger tournament. He agreed, though, that the time and distance involved in playing a doubleheader in Oklahoma City meant a long day. Monroe's natural position was shortstop, but he could play third base just as well. I told him we would probably need him at second or third in Oklahoma because Fat was firmly entrenched at short and refused to give up that position.

Sam and T. J. were supposed to pitch the first game for us, but they didn't show up, so I got an unexpected start for game one of the doubleheader. I had planned on pitching that day, but the idea of pitching two games did not appeal to me. I hoped the other pitchers would arrive soon.

The Braves had some great players, and we struggled to win the first game, 2–1. When our other two pitchers still had not appeared, Mr. Sedberry tried to get Fat to pitch the second game. He refused. Mr. Sedberry looked around for another pitcher, and his eye fell on Monroe.

"Mr. Craft, does your friend pitch?" he asked me.

"Yes, but he doesn't enjoy pitching as much as he does playing infield. Why don't you let me start, and let's hope relief shows up soon," I told him.

"Are you sure, Mr. Craft?" he asked.

"I'll go as far as I can, Mr. Sedberry," I told him. "Maybe someone will show up after we get the second game started." Both of us doubted this because it was already late afternoon.

When I finally signaled Mr. Sedberry to the mound two hours later, I was struggling. We were seven innings into the second game and trailing 1–2. He motioned toward Fat and Monroe, and they joined us on the mound.

"Fat, I need you to pitch the rest of the game. We'll move

Mo from second base to shortstop. Mr. Craft can take third base," Mr. Sedberry told them.

Fat flat refused. He crossed his arms, stuck his nose in the air, and told us he would not do it.

I don't think Fat's refusal was racially motivated. This was not a black-white confrontation for the Stars. Instead, Fat considered himself the reigning king at shortstop, and I believe he probably feared a person of Monroe's talent, regardless of his color, might threaten his throne. Fat was a very good pitcher, and in other circumstances he would have grudgingly agreed to relieve me in a second game of a doubleheader, but with Monroe there, the situation was very different.

I looked around, not knowing what to do. "I have nothing left," I told the men on the mound. "Someone is going to have to pitch." I staggered wearily off the mound and toward third base. A smattering of applause followed me.

"I'll do it," Monroe volunteered. And that is how Monroe became the Stars' second white pitcher for one game. He didn't pitch often, but at that point he could throw harder than I could.

As Monroe recalls it, he was pitching for the Stars not because he was good at it but because he knew how. Mr. Sedberry brought him in because we were out of options. Mo didn't pitch regularly, so he didn't practice it, and he was uncomfortable stepping into a game as a pitcher when he had not worked out at that position. He was too much of a competitor to tolerate doing a bad job, but he was willing to do it for the team.

Monroe held his own that day by preventing the Braves from scoring, but we could not put any players across the plate, losing the game 1–2. Interestingly, I was both the winning and the losing pitcher on the same day. I pitched sixteen innings that day, a personal record I did not care to repeat. Before the long ride home, we told Mr. Sedberry that we could not play any more doubleheaders if we didn't have enough players.

Late in July we played the Sheppard Air Force team at their base in Wichita Falls. Their personnel changed with every game as troops were deployed, but their teams were always all white. They did not have a separate black ball club like Fort Wolters did. I don't know why because we saw some black men in air force uniforms in Wichita Falls. However, at that time the army no doubt recruited black combat soldiers in greater numbers than the air force recruited black airmen.

Sheppard's baseball team never attracted large crowds. Airmen who might have the day off preferred to do other things with their Sundays than watch baseball. Our fans were welcome at the games, but sometimes the APs, "Air Police"—the equivalent of the military's MPs—would question our fans as they tried to enter the base. Despite this treatment, the environment at Sheppard was far less hostile than at Bowie.

With the Civil Rights Movement beginning, security was getting tighter at the military bases than Mr. Sedberry had ever seen. When our team arrived at the gate, we were wearing our uniforms, but the APs asked us for our driver's licenses and recorded the numbers. The APs then gave us directions to the field, pointed us toward the ball park, and waved us in. Their reaction to us was neither warm nor cool. They were just doing their job.

When a large caravan of our fans showed up, the APs were not as receptive. A new shift of APs had started and had no idea a black baseball team was playing that day. Several cars full of black people arriving simultaneously made them nervous, and after much explanation and a few phone calls, the fans were allowed inside.

Our fans were not pleased that they had been delayed, but they had spent all of their lives being treated as second-class citizens. They did not waste a lot of time complaining about it or resenting their treatment. They had, in many ways, come to expect it.

Once the fans arrived at the baseball field, they were disappointed by its appearance. Home plate faced north and the outfield fences were wire, so our batters would have the sun in their eyes and our outfielders could not chase down long fly balls or have them bounce off a fence and back into play. At least there were lights, which meant our fans could watch the end of the game if it ran late. Another bonus was that very few white civilian fans had arrived, giving our fans greater freedom in selecting where they wanted to sit.

Sheppard had a junk ball pitcher from New Jersey named Bombeck. None of us could hit him. He kept us off balance the whole day. All we could do was swing and miss, but I was really pitching well. I struck out twenty-three men and we won 2–1. That was the most men I'd ever struck out in one game. The next time we played there, we found out the air force had transferred Bombeck, and we were grateful!

The weeks that followed involved several losses that I'd prefer not to recall because I didn't enjoy losing, but one game was memorable because I received a standing ovation, my first ever. We were on the road for a game against the Pied Pipers, an all-black team from Hamlin, northwest of Abilene and more than two hours away from Wichita Falls. We played Hamlin on the white high school's diamond, which featured below-ground dugouts that had concrete roofs. The field faced south. Black and white teams in Hamlin both used the field, but at separate times. For Hamlin's game against the Stars, a large, all-black crowd filled the stands, about half of them from Graham and Wichita Falls.

I threw a dropping curve to the leadoff batter, and he popped it up about halfway down the third-base line, too far for the catcher or third baseman to field, but just across from my position as pitcher. As I sprinted toward the weak pop-up and dove for the foul ball, I miraculously caught it and slid into the Hamlin dugout. In the confusion, I briefly lost sight of the ball but held it against my chest with my glove and bare right hand.

The Hamlin players also caught me during my unexpected journey into their dugout. I lay across a row of players as the umpire ran over and descended into the dugout to ask, "Well, did he catch it?"

"He did," one of the Hamlin players said, "and it was one hell of a catch!"

The umpire called the out while the Hamlin players dusted me off. I emerged from the dugout with the ball, and our fans rose to their feet in applause. I was startled by the standing ovation and stood there for a moment not knowing how to react.

I thought I should do something, so I did what most players do. I took off my cap and waved it toward them. When I did that, the Hamlin side also rose and applauded. I then realized to that baseball crowd it didn't make any difference what color I was. If a player made a great play, they appreciated and applauded it.

We easily defeated the Pied Pipers, and, as we gathered in

the parking lot for some tailgating, the Hamlin manager came over and shook my hand. All of us were visiting, and the manager asked me, "What's your name, white boy?"

I told him my name and where I was from.

"You're OK," he told me. He then told me that after I had made my catch in his team's dugout and was walking back to the mound, he told his team, "We're going to have our hands full with that white boy today."

"How do you know that?" one of his players had asked.

"A pitcher who will go to such lengths to catch a foul ball will find a way to beat you. That white boy is a winner!"

I thanked him. I was touched by his sincere praise. I still remember his kindness. Baseball fans know and appreciate good plays and players, even when they're on the other team and beat their home team. That is why at today's ball games I still hear a smattering of applause from the home side when the visitors make a great play. Those few claps are the home fans who are true fans of the game, recognizing a job well done.

At the end of July, we were scheduled to play against an all-black team from Stamford, an old cowboy town about two and a half hours west of Jacksboro. The Stamford baseball field was part of the town's rodeo arena. Both football and baseball games were held there, with the baseball diamond positioned at an angle in the elongated arena. Those were tough games because we played on dirt. I don't suppose small towns play baseball in rodeo arenas anymore, but they did at that time to save money. The arenas had parking, lighting, bleachers, rest rooms, and concession stands. The only thing missing, really, was grass.

I met Mr. Sedberry at the Graham courthouse for our

carpool to Stamford. He told me his car wouldn't start, so he rode with me. He was in an unusually somber mood, and I thought his car trouble had caused it.

"Have you been reading about Martin Luther King's work in Atlanta?" he suddenly asked me.

"Yes, I have," I replied, surprised at his choice of topic for conversation.

"What do you think about it?" he asked.

"I don't think I quite know yet," I said.

"Yes, you do," he corrected me. Our conversation had ended as quickly as it had begun. In retrospect, I think Mr. Sedberry wanted me to understand that my experiences with the Stars had made me a more compassionate person. I had experienced firsthand what my teammates' lives were like. We sat in silence for the remainder of the drive to Stamford.

The Bulldogs didn't have much on the field that day. I don't recall many of the details of our game against them, but as I was sitting next to Mr. Sedberry on the bench, I casually commented to him that their pitcher wasn't any good. I thought about this for a few minutes and then asked him, "Why do we see so few good black pitchers?"

Mr. Sedberry suddenly became more talkative that half inning than he had been all day, and his words have remained with me over the years.

"I don't know," he responded. "That's why we have you."

"I appreciate that, but really, we have other athletes on our team who have the talent to play anywhere on the field, like Fat, Rabbit, and Bobby."

"Well, I believe our team lacks discipline, and pitchers need a lot of discipline," he said.

"That's interesting. Give me an example."

"I'll give you a good one," he said. "If you were manager, what would you do right now?" he asked, sweeping his arm in the direction of the field. "Look at our positions. What would you do?"

I stood up and easily read our offense. "OK, we have Rabbit on first, nobody out, and a weak hitter at the plate. I'd bunt," I said.

"Exactly," he said.

"Then why don't we?" I asked. He and I then laughed as we both remembered our disastrous experiment with the bunt sign during the previous season.

Mr. Sedberry explained to me why the Stars wouldn't bunt so that I would stop second-guessing his strategies. He told me, "Mr. Craft, your teammates don't want to bunt. They want to hit home runs. You, on the other hand, have more discipline in your right arm than my entire team does. Does that mean we want to play on white teams? No, we don't. We may have some talent, but you have discipline, and I believe it's hard for a black team to acquire self-discipline."

"Whoa, Mr. Sedberry. I'm not just a white player. We're a team, and we're playing together," I said.

"You, Mr. Craft, are an exception. You are on the team, but if you were black, I think you'd be just as undisciplined as the rest of us."

I found this idea interesting, and, when I pressed him for more evidence, he said, "I'm talking about if Fat or Rabbit played with an all-white team like Bobby did, then they would have to play by the white team's rules in front of white fans. In essence, we would have to be white ballplayers. We are not, and we don't want to be. We like the way we play the game," he said.

"That will change, Mr. Sedberry. You know it will," I said. "This is a great game that always changes and adapts. It was a very different game years ago, and it will be a very different game years from now. Recognizable, but different.

Games that don't adapt don't survive. I'd rather have a different game than none at all."

"I guess so, Mr. Craft. But I would hate to lose our game. You see, integration just scares the hell out of me. On the one hand, I certainly want years of injustice righted. On the other hand, though, I'm frightened my team and even our whole race will lose its identity. And what about fun? Do you think that any of us would have this much fun if one of us were playing on an all-white team?"

"No, I don't at all," I said. "I've never had this much fun playing ball, so I can see that."

"Well, let me tell you something. I don't buy the line that Jackie Robinson and some of the other guys who have quit black baseball to join the major leagues did it to break a color barrier. They did it strictly for the money. Don't be fooled by the color line. I think they've sold out because they've destroyed black baseball as we know and love it. I wouldn't want to play with white people."

"Hey," I reminded him, "I'm a whitey."

"No, no, no," he said. "I'm talking about an all-white team. If a few of the Stars played on your team, then we'd have to try to be white, and we're not, and we don't want that." And with that observation he became quiet again.

"All right," I said. There was really nothing else for me to do but agree with him. He had said what was on his mind, and he had a right to say it.

We were silent through the rest of the game and left the tailgating early together. He said nothing for a long time in the car but then commented, "Well, I kind of unloaded on you today." I said nothing.

"I've never talked to a white man like that before. I hope I didn't offend you," he added.

"No, you didn't. But I was wondering, what brought all this up?" I asked.

After a long pause, he asked if we had any beer in the car. It was a road trip, so naturally we did. He opened us both a can, then another. "I was reading about Martin Luther King's work. Instead of being indignant about the abuse those folks in Atlanta were suffering, you know what I was thinking, Mr. Craft?"

"I have no idea," I said.

He grinned and slapped me on the back. "I thought about our wonderful two Fourth of July celebrations with our Windthorst friends, about black and white children playing together, about our fans eating, drinking, and visiting together. I thought especially about how both teams appreciated how well we all played baseball together as athletes and men. I think that will end soon."

"Why?" I asked. "I'll bet we'll host them next year in Graham."

"No," he said. "With integration forced on Graham, the town won't want to acknowledge Juneteenth and may even be afraid to celebrate it." Mr. Sedberry was prophetic again, for that is exactly what happened.

Mr. Sedberry heaved his beer can out the window with a sigh and said, "And what the hell do I have in common with a northern nigger?" he sighed.

The question made me jump. "What do you mean?" I asked him.

"Mr. Craft, most of the civil rights leaders I read about are from the North, and I have little in common with them other than the color of my skin. To me, they are outsiders to the South as much as black ballplayers are outsiders to the white major leagues," he said.

I knew Mr. Sedberry revered the Negro Leagues and was grieving their demise. I recognized his despair in their disappearance. I didn't have the heart to remind him that Rosa Parks, Martin Luther King, and Thurgood Marshall were from the South. Mr. Sedberry recognized that there would be a price to pay for the integration of major league baseball, but how could a player or fan truly be compensated for the loss of an entire league and its teams, the Homestead Grays, the Kansas City Monarchs, the Birmingham Black Barons, the Newark Eagles, the Baltimore Elites, the Baltimore Black Sox, the New York Cubans, the Cleveland Buckeyes, the Philadelphia Stars, Chicago's American Giants, and the Indianapolis Clowns?

"Mr. Sedberry, don't you think organized baseball's integration is good for this country?" I asked.

"Mr. Craft, I love the Negro Leagues. Where are all those players going to play? Where are the fans going to see a good game? It's great to see Jackie Robinson play, but with his success, the other major league teams have raided the Negro Leagues for some of their finest players," he said.

"Don't they now have the opportunity to play for a major league team, though?" I asked.

"Not always," he said. "The major leagues harm baseball when they bring gifted black players out of the Negro Leagues and leave them in the minor leagues." Mr. Sedberry then explained to me that white players already held many key major-league positions, and the new black players often languished in the white minors under conditions not much better than in the Negro Leagues, though the white minor leagues might offer better salaries. The black players were away from their homes and fans, with little hope of ever playing major-league ball. They were, in effect, warehoused, probably without their knowledge.

"It's a process," I said as I tried to console Mr. Sedberry. "Even good white players spend a long time waiting their turn to play in the majors. Look at how far we've come. Black fans are now attending major-league games. They'll see their favorite players in action and want to know how they measure up against white major leaguers."

"I don't care. I already know how they measure up. I'm a manager and a fan," he said.

He had seen the black owners of the Negro League teams fight failing attendance, struggle to make payrolls, and sell off their stars to survive. The end was inevitable. A few teams like the Monarchs and the Clowns hung around until the mid-1960s by barnstorming, touring the country without an organized league, but the glory days of Mr. Sedberry's beloved black ball were gone.

The uncertain future of the black baseball player who no longer had a black league to call home frustrated Mr. Sedberry. He and I didn't know that an unwritten quota system on the number of black players on each major-league team probably existed. In Brad Snyder's highly informative *Beyond the Shadow of the Senators: The Untold Story of the Homestead Grays and the Integration of Baseball* (2004), players claim that four or five black men on one team would have been too many.

Whether black players were warehoused or were the victims of an unfair quota system, Mr. Sedberry had good reason to be frustrated with their lack of progress through the minor leagues and their inability to choose where they would play once they joined a major-league team. Others also shared Mr. Sedberry's distaste for the injustices players suffered in organized baseball, eventually including major leaguer Curt Flood. Flood challenged the "reserve clause" system when he did not want to be traded from the St. Louis Cardinals to the Philadelphia Phillies after the 1969 season. He fought for his rights to be a free agent in the U.S. Supreme Court case *Flood v. Kuhn*, which, while not successful, moved the legal system forward to abolish the reserve clause and establish free agency by 1975.

Flood, who challenged as great an injustice as Jackie Robinson did, was never as celebrated as his predecessor. Robinson had told *The Sporting News* on November 1, 1945, that he was "ready to take the chance. Maybe I'm doing something for my race," but Mr. Sedberry strongly disagreed with him. He had a comic expression for what he considered to be bullshit. He clapped his hands to each side of his face, widened his eyes, and shouted, "Sho 'nuff?" He felt that the black players who left the Negro Leagues for Major League Baseball were "traitors to their race."

I disagreed with him.

"How else were they ever going to become major leaguers and prove that they were athletes equal to or better than white players?" I asked him.

"White boy, they already were," he replied rather testily.

"You, as a black man, believe that, but the white man sure doesn't," I said.

"Why would I care what they believe anyway? If I believe what some of them do—that I'm not any better than a farm animal—then how could a farm animal possibly play such a beautiful game so well?"

NINE
The Last Inning

TEXAS IN JULY CAN BE A CRUEL PLACE, the sun and heat bearing down on grass, livestock, and baseball teams. Although July 1960 was especially difficult for me and the Stars, the reason we struggled had nothing to do with the weather. When Mr. Sedberry made his weekly call to me to let me know when, where, and what time we were playing, I received a terrible shock. His voice wavered over the phone line as he asked if Monroe and Tony would try to be there. I told him I didn't know. Then he hesitated and added, "If you know of a white catcher, we could sure use one."

"Why?" I asked.

"You see, Emmitt was killed this week in a car wreck," he said.

I suddenly realized we had lost two catchers in two years to car accidents. I knew instantly that the fate of the Stars was sealed. I don't recall the team we played that Sunday, but I do remember that we lost badly.

When I first arrived at the field, Rabbit took me aside.

"Did you know Emmitt was killed in a car wreck in East Texas?" he asked. Our eyes met.

"Yes. Mr. Sedberry told me over the phone," I said. "Why didn't you call me to let me know when the funeral was?"

He shrugged his shoulders.

"Did you attend it?" I asked.

"Sure."

We were still living in totally different, segregated worlds. They didn't think that I would want to know about Emmitt's death, and that hurt. While we had shared experiences on the ball field, during road trips, and while tailgating after the game, I recognized that I wasn't a part of their regular daily lives nor they of mine. I was hardly a passing thought to them, other than on game days when they wondered if their white boy would pitch for them. Asking a white man to attend a black man's funeral probably did not cross their minds. Even though I was his teammate, they probably didn't think it was appropriate for them to call me or for me to attend.

"This is going to be the end of the Stars," I told him.

"Yeah, we lost a really good catcher back when Alfred died. Emmitt wasn't as good, but he was dependable. Mr. Sedberry's been shaking the bushes to find us another good catcher," Rabbit said.

I glanced at home plate to see that our starting catcher was none other than old "Toothless" Tommy Jones, the same catcher who two years before sang to me and complained to Mr. Sedberry when my curve ball damaged his baseball-weary knees. Tommy had not caught me in over a year, and his baseball skills had certainly not improved during his time off.

"I guess he hasn't been shaking them hard enough," I told Rabbit as I headed for the bullpen.

The team rapidly fell apart. In addition to catching, Emmitt had served as team co-captain with Rabbit. After church on Sunday Emmitt and Rabbit had rounded up all our ballplayers for the games. Together, they knew everyone's habits and hideouts. Without their organizing us, the wonderful world of Stars baseball was no longer fun.

I wondered then and still do why the Stars didn't call me about our teammates' funerals. Years later, when Fisher and Bobby Lee Herron died, I saw the obituaries and locations of the funerals in the Wichita Falls newspaper. I attended them. I was only one of two white people at each service, the only Star there. The congregants at the services made me feel as comfortable and as welcome in their black churches as I had felt at their baseball games.

In the summer of 2003, I missed a call from Mary Alice Sedberry, Mr. Sedberry's wife. She had left a message that Mr. Sedberry was ailing and didn't have much time. He wanted to see me, but I didn't get the message until it was too late because I was working at my ranch in New Mexico. I regret that I didn't have the chance to say good-bye.

Mr. Sedberry died on August 19, 2003, in Graham, Texas. He was survived by his wife, seven daughters, four sons, twenty-three grandchildren, and thirty-seven great-grandchildren. A large crowd, both black and white, attended the funeral at Trinity Christian Center Church in Graham. Mr. Sedberry was well respected by his community. Rabbit was a pallbearer, and we talked for a long time at Pioneer Cemetery following the burial.

We discussed the end of the last season, how even Mr. Sedberry was pressed into service, usually in the infield. While Mr. Sedberry certainly knew what to do intellectually, he was not gifted enough athletically to make much difference. He would take off his tie and coat, but he played in slacks, a white dress shirt, and dress shoes because we had no spare uniforms. Each player had been fitted for his own uniform, and if that particular player were a no-show, then the uniform hung useless in his closet. While this was disappointing to Mr. Sedberry, he never lost faith in his team and those of us who truly cared about the game.

During our seasons together, I never thought about someday attending my teammates' funerals, though in 1960 I realized our playing days were numbered. The Stars' attendance became so sporadic that for several games late in our last summer together we would drag fans out of the stands to play in their thin slacks and shirts. I would turn around on the mound and see two or three fans we had pulled out of the stands so that we could have nine players on the field. Any hopes of recruiting additional players, white or black, were dashed that late in the season. Good players were already playing for other teams and could not be convinced to join a losing one. With our losing record, team morale sank.

We were just a shell of the great club we once were. Mr. Sedberry continued to try, but he could not recruit anyone. Even black teenagers were not tempted. They had begged us to give them a chance in 1959 when we were winning and had an adequate number of good players. Then everyone wanted a chance to play with the Stars, but not now. The once mighty Stars were fading.

I was becoming very unhappy with our team, and Mr. Sedberry knew it. He promised me that we would improve. Our next game was against Anna at Trinity Park in Fort Worth.

The park, on the west side of University Boulevard, was owned by Fort Worth's Parks and Recreation Department. Both black and white teams used the field at different times. The city charged us a small fee to play there because both of our teams were from out of town.

Before the game, Mr. Sedberry told me, "One of the best black outfielders I've seen in some time is going to join us. He catches balls with a basket catch, just like Willie Mays."

Catching a ball at waist level didn't seem like such a good idea to me, but we really needed some help. Tony and Monroe had already given up on us. I was close to quitting, too, so I told Mr. Sedberry that I really hoped the new player would help us.

Anna had a good all-black ball club, and when they got on base, they quickly learned they could steal every base off old Tommy, the toothless catcher. By the fifth inning, I had already struck out six batters, but the bases were still loaded. Tommy was dropping the third strike and seemed worn out. Mr. Sedberry called time. He came to the mound to tell me the good news.

"Mr. Craft," he said. "That great outfielder I was telling you about is here. I'm going to put him in left field."

"I wish he were a catcher," I said.

The young man dashed onto the field. He wore a bright red uniform with "Red Devils" across the back of his jersey. He was extremely excited, and I couldn't tell if he was naturally or unnaturally high. He rushed to the mound to introduce himself as the next Willie Mays.

"All you have to do to win this game is let Anna hit everything to me," he said.

I wasn't one for showboat moves like basket catches, but Willie Mays had made them his trademark. His coaches had long ago quit asking him to stop catching balls in such a risky fashion. However, the fans had come to love and expect the spectacular catches.

As fate and the gods of baseball decreed, the next Anna batter lofted my curve ball to "Willie Jr." He hovered under the ball and pounded his glove, shouting, "It's mine! It's mine!"

Holding his glove and right hand at his waist, he prepared to show us his stuff. The baseball hit him squarely on top of his head. It didn't carom off at an angle but bounced twenty feet straight up in the air. America's future superstar lay spread-eagled and unconscious as four runners laughingly circled the bases and scored.

I watched as our players tried to revive the new left fielder, then I turned and walked to our dugout. Curiously, I didn't think my baseball career would end like this, an uneventful regular-season game. Like most athletes, I had envisioned a no-hitter or a championship game as my last time on the field.

I thought about what I would do next. My life without the Stars flashed briefly through my mind. I would probably go back to full-time ranching. We had only played games on Wednesday nights in Graham and Sunday afternoons in Spudder Park in Wichita Falls or on the road, so I had been ranching the entire time I played for the Stars anyway.

I knew I would never see them play again. I had no desire to watch their continued demise. I disliked participating in the team's downfall, and I didn't want to watch them from the stands.

I remember Tony and Monroe asking me why I stayed on the team as long as I did. They couldn't understand why I continued to play for the Stars when we started losing nearly every game. Toward the end of the second season, I pitched for them because I had been a very loyal friend to Mr. Sedberry and Rabbit, and I really liked my teammates. I also knew when I walked away from them that I would be giving up a game I loved.

By late in my second season with the Stars, my family, even my father, had become ambivalent about my playing "black ball." My quitting the team would be rather anticlimactic to them.

I picked up my warm-up jacket and extended my hand to Mr. Sedberry. He shook it, and I gave him a hug.

"Mr. Sedberry, it's been a real ride, but this is it," I said.

"No, just give us one more chance, Mr. Craft," he said.

"I can't do that. It's not fun anymore," I told him. I told everyone good-bye. In July 1960, I walked away from the Stars and baseball forever.

Later Rabbit told me that Mr. Sedberry had a hard time breaking the news of my departure to the team. Rabbit recalled, "The next week, Mr. Sedberry tells me, 'You know, Mr. Craft won't be back anymore.' I wanted to know why. Mr. Sedberry said, 'He's just kind of fed up with the team. The players are not showing up on time, and they're leaving us in a bind. He drives over from Jacksboro, and there are no players.'"

I knew that Rabbit continued playing for the Stars after I quit, but the team was never the same. They never found a replacement for me. Rabbit later told me, "You was a part of our team, and when you left, we wasn't quite as strong. We played, but it just didn't seem like we were together. After the 1960 season ended, I gave up baseball." When we started that season, we never thought it would be our last.

Mr. Sedberry remained the coach. He later told me, "When you quit, that was the end of the Stars. I knew I would never have another team like them, but I wanted to continue coaching. That kind of team, if you are lucky, only happens once in a lifetime. I was lucky."

The Stars folded three years after my departure, ending ten years of local all-black league baseball in Wichita Falls and Graham. Mr. Sedberry fought to keep the tradition alive by forming an independent team of young black players called the Graham Junkyard Dogs in 1963. He recruited teenagers from Graham for his new team because they were more available for games and were more consistent in their attendance at games and practices than the Stars had been. The teenagers really wanted to play ball, and Mr. Sedberry could count on them to show up.

Mr. Sedberry coached semi-professional baseball until 1971. He thoroughly enjoyed baseball, and instead of being discouraged by the disappearance of the Stars, he used his time to introduce the game to the next generation of players. He later told me the Junkyard Dogs didn't possess the same talent and didn't win many games, but being their coach was very rewarding. They wanted to learn and were very serious about playing baseball. Mr. Sedberry gave the gift of baseball to the young people in his community, and I will always be grateful to him for giving the gift of the Stars to me.

EPILOGUE

As I become older, events from fifty years ago seem so distant that I begin to question how they really happened. Other times, games from my 1959 and 1960 seasons with the Stars seem as vivid as yesterday. I never thought my experiences were newsworthy until 1993, when Hollace Weiner of the *Fort Worth Star-Telegram* called me to ask about my involvement in the West Texas Colored League.

"Did this all truly happen?" she asked me.

"Yes," I told her. "It did, but no one has ever been interested in it."

Hollace had been covering a story on my sister, and Linda had told her, "If you want a really good story, talk to my brother."

I spoke with Hollace a few times on the phone, but at first I refused to give her a formal interview because I was very busy with my civic duties, my ranch, and my family, and I didn't think anyone would want to read about my baseball experiences. They were so long ago. She called several more times. Then a few days later a photographer for the *Star-Telegram* walked into my office unannounced. Hollace joined him and said, "If you want to throw me out of your office, you certainly can, but I just have to do this story."

I laughed. I was totally unprepared to talk to her, but I told her, "If you are that passionate about this story, let's do it."

Her story awoke memories that I had long forgotten. I started to wonder where my former teammates and friends were. I don't know why I had never tried to contact them. We had gone our separate ways. We married, had children, and pursued careers. We were busy living our lives.

During those years, the sport remained important to me. I loved watching baseball on TV and reading about it in the newspapers. Of course I became a fan of the Texas Rangers and at one time had season tickets. I also coached my two sons and my daughter in Little League and helped with many other Little League teams for more than twenty years. I loved watching the children play all the positions on the field. We had fun, and they, hopefully, picked up some degree of expertise in baseball. I knew older students could enjoy baseball, too, and as a member of the Board of Regents at Midwestern State University in Wichita Falls, I helped restore varsity baseball to the university in 1982.

My love for baseball also helped me create a unique business opportunity for myself. In 1964, I realized that fans would watch their favorite baseball teams on TV in their homes if they could. I started a business that delivered cable television, and baseball games, to small Texas communities like mine. My business partners were John Campbell from Irving and Texas State Senator Tom Creighton of Mineral Wells. I eventually bought them out and continued to build cable systems for towns surrounding Jacksboro. I was elected president of the Texas Cable Television Association in

1983 and 1984 and later elected to represent the small cable TV systems of America as director of the National Cable TV Association in Washington, D.C. In 1988 I was elected to the National Cable TV Pioneers Hall of Fame.

Senator Creighton, then my closest friend and mentor, introduced me to the political world. He represented District 22, a large area encompassing counties northwest, west, and southwest of Fort Worth. His district comprised eighteen rural counties, the second largest district in the state next to the one from Harris County in Houston. Delegates from each county elect state committee chairs at the state convention to represent them. In 1966, with the senator's urging and help, I decided to run for the office of Senatorial District Committee Chair for District 22.

At that time I was the youngest chair ever elected, and I served six two-year terms, more terms than anyone in history. I held the position until 1978. During that time I had the honor of working with Texas governors Conally, Smith, and Briscoe. In 1970 the state was in the process of redistricting, redrawing the voting lines so that the state's voter distribution, by factors like population density and race, would be represented equally in Austin.

Redistricting was just as controversial then as it is now. To Senator Creighton's amazement and disgust, his beloved District 22 was dismantled. We were only allowed to keep ten rural counties, including my Jack County, in our district plus the southern half of Tarrant County. The shift represented the urbanization of Texas, and leaders like me had to represent voters from cities in addition to those from the country. In many instances, the rural leaders were simply replaced by urban ones.

The Dallas–Fort Worth metropolitan area suddenly became important to me and the Senator. Parker and Johnson counties touch southern Tarrant County, whose county seat is Fort Worth. Because Parker and Johnson counties were part of the former District 22, we unexpectedly received a portion of Fort Worth in the new District 22.

Senator Don Kennard, a liberal Democrat, originally represented the southern section of Fort Worth. He lived in north Fort Worth, though, and suddenly his district was reduced to the northern half of Tarrant County, a very conservative area.

Senator Creighton, probably the most conservative Democratic senator in Texas, received east and southeast Fort Worth, where Senator Kennard's most loyal and vocal supporters lived. This disturbing reversal of political philosophies frustrated the minority populations, including members of the labor unions, who were now being represented by Senator Creighton. He deeply disliked any kind of labor union, vowing that he would never put a branch office in Fort Worth and refusing to meet with union and minority leaders. The tense situation showed no signs of resolution.

I had no experience dealing with unions but found their leaders, Garland and Lois Hamm and Frank Barron, to be good people. They had been elected to represent their fellow workers' interests, just as I had been elected to be an advocate for my district. I also found many of the minority women and pastors in the new District 22 to be very helpful. The younger people, though, wanted every political concession, even the ones over which I had no control. Senator Creighton refused to meet with any of them, so I formed an alliance with the labor union leaders. I trusted them, and they always kept their word. They fought among themselves, but not with me.

My base of operations became the Fort Worth Petroleum Club. I joined even though I wasn't a resident of Fort Worth so that I could meet with the senator's constituents there. The club was segregated at that time but permitted our meetings. I thought that was a step in the right direction for them, one they did not have to take.

During one Saturday afternoon meeting, the older black leaders were trying to calm the younger ones while shouts of "Uncle Tom" rose from the back of the room. I looked around and suddenly flashed back to my first game with the Stars at Spudder Park. Once again, mine was the only white face.

I stood, knowing that I had an experience few white men ever had. Why had I not thought of it before? One particularly vocal man from the back saw me and yelled, "What is that white guy doing here?"

"He sure as hell ain't the janitor," was the muffled response, followed by a few chuckles.

All heads turned to me, and I responded, "I understand where you all are coming from." Derisive laughter came from the back, where many college students sat.

"Let me tell you a story," I said.

"Listen up, folks. This man is trying to speak," an older gentleman said politely.

"I was the first white man to play in the West Texas Colored League." There was silence. I had their attention, but then I thought, where the hell am I going with this?

I wove a story with the fabric of teamwork, conflict, mutual respect, and friendship that the Stars had given me. I told them what we accomplished as teammates, especially when my white friends Tony and Monroe joined us for games.

At the end of my story, I looked into the eyes of both groups. I could see no change in the older people, but I saw something different in the young. I jumped at what I perceived to be the opportunity to unite the factions.

"I will always be honest with you. I will represent your views; however, you have to work with me. Remember, the ten rural counties that are in your new district, though their role is diminished, can still outvote you. They will do it if you demand concessions I can't produce. You and they have to be represented percentagewise, just like all the other districts in Texas. Further, if you want to fight with me and antagonize me, I can assure you that none of you will get a damn thing done. I can't put it any plainer."

After my speech, we slowly started working together. The turnaround was very much like my years with the Stars. For a while, I met with the Fort Worth groups separately. At the State Conventions, just as in the baseball stands, the representatives from Fort Worth sat apart from the rural representatives, but I could tell that they were starting to respect each other and perhaps were even starting to like each other. We still had our differences, but when it came time to vote on an issue, we were all Democrats.

After the *Star-Telegram*'s interview, I started searching for my old teammates. Some of them I only knew by first name. I found Mr. Sedberry first, right where he had always been, on Lincoln Street in Graham. He was still married to Mary.

Mr. Sedberry and I had lunch in Graham and Jacksboro, and my old manager tried to recall where the other players were. We were helped by Channel 8, the local ABC affiliate, and its sport editor, John Pronk, who found Bobby Lee Herron and Clarence "Rabbit" Myles. John asked them to come to Jacksboro, and he produced a documentary on our team's playing days.

Rabbit had remained in touch with the guys, many of whom had already died. Rabbit asked Earnest "Fat" Locke to breakfast, and we met him in Wichita Falls. I told them I wanted to write about our experiences before I forgot them. We began to meet regularly and compare memories. The more we met and talked, the more we remembered, though we didn't always agree on a particular event. Now, only Monroe, Rabbit, and I are left.

During our breakfast meetings, Rabbit, Fat, and I discussed all the changes in baseball we've seen from our sandlot days to the current Little Leagues. We agreed we had a lot more fun, but the kids we see today are technically superior because they have adult coaches and access to instructional videos, baseball camps, and other such opportunities. Children now are also much stronger and bigger than we were at that age. We lamented the loss of town teams and semi-pro baseball that had been a way of life for seventy-five years in the small towns around Graham and Jacksboro. Those games had been the one thing to do on the weekends. Monroe and Rabbit had watched that way of life die, too.

As a pioneer in the cable television industry, I recognized my ironic role in the decline of our town teams as my business brought far-away games to our small towns. In the 1960s we started watching the New York Yankees on our home television screens, in the comfort of our living rooms, drinking beer from our refrigerators, and eating frozen dinners on TV trays. Who needed the town teams like the Jacksboro Roughnecks or Midway Falcons when such luxury was available in the air-conditioned comfort of home?

A televised game with the camera's focus of pitcher-hitter-catcher is not the same as being outside on a beautiful night, watching an entire team play. At a live game I can see the whole team, its defensive alignments, the signs from the coaches, the chattering and cheers of the fans, and the beautiful women in the stands. No play-by-play or color commentary will tell me what I already know about baseball because I played it.

During the past several years, I've been fascinated with the revival of town baseball in Fort Worth and northern Texas. Beginning in 2001 with the return of the Fort Worth Cats as an independent team and continuing with the start of the Texas Collegiate League in 2004, baseball in Texas has come full circle. The Cats trace their history to the Fort Worth Panthers, who began play in 1888 and were the Brooklyn Dodgers' Double-A farm club from 1926 to 1964. They played north of the Tarrant County Courthouse in Fort Worth at LaGrave Field, which was rebuilt in 2002, with home plate in its original place.

In the summer of 2006, the Graham Roughnecks played in the Texas Collegiate League, and I attended some of their games. Their owner, Frank Beaman, is my friend. We watched college baseball players sharpen their skills against teams from Mineral Wells, Granbury, Weatherford, Plano, McKinney, Coppell, and Colleyville. Teams have players from across the country, including the Ivy League, California, and the Big 12 Conference. The college players use wooden bats to give themselves major-league practice and to gain the attention of professional scouts. Local families serve as hosts for the players, who live in the families' homes. Some of the players work part-time jobs in their adopted towns when they are not playing baseball.

Because the college students become such a special part of the community while they play on their teams, fans develop town cheers, celebrate players' birthdays, hold church nights and Lion's Club nights at the baseball field, set off fireworks, and provide home cooking in the stands. Players toss water balloons at the crowd between innings, and children run wild on the field after games. The local families are cheering members of their own community and households, which makes it very much like town ball.

Still, there is a difference. I know the original town teams did not approach the quality of play I see in the Cats or the Texas Collegiate League, but the players on the first town teams were permanent residents. Fans knew them all and went to church with them. The players were barbers, pharmacists, school teachers, ranchers, and friends. Fans praised them or ribbed them after the game or the next day on the street. Fans and players had a sense of ownership over their own team, a sense of ownership that no longer exists. They were never great players, but they did their best, just like the rest of us. Although the original town teams are gone, I'm glad a new version of them continues in the form of independent teams and summer baseball for college students.

While I appreciate how baseball evolves, I also enjoy remembering the past. Southwestern Bell sponsored the African American History Month Family Day and Negro League Baseball Reunion at the African American Museum at Fair Park in Dallas on February 20, 1999. Mr. Sedberry, Fat, Rabbit, and I were invited to participate in the activities, which began at noon with a luncheon. We were to travel together from Jacksboro to Dallas for the event, but Fat backed out at the last minute. He wasn't feeling well.

I was impressed with the museum. I never even knew it existed. It had uniforms from every baseball team in the Negro Leagues, plus many photos of their great players. After a few speeches, thirteen former baseball players, including me, participated in a roundtable discussion led by Larry Lester. Larry was the director of research at the Negro Leagues Baseball Museum in Kansas City, Missouri.

Shacka Jones and Walter Day, cochairs of the Friends of the Texas Sports History African American Museum, introduced us. Former players from both Texas and Louisiana filled the stage: William Blair, Frank Ensley, Mamie Johnson (the only surviving woman player), John Miles, Bertrand Patterson, Charles Wills, Henry Francis, N. J. Jones, James McGee, Alex Trigg, J. W. Wright, Mr. Sedberry, Rabbit, and yours truly, Jerry Craft.

The very first question from the audience to me was, "What are you doing here?"

There were a few chuckles from the crowd, and then I told my story. I explained how I first joined the Stars and how the Abilene Blues' batters stood on home plate during my first game. I answered a lot of questions. Some of the players around me spoke eloquently about their experiences. Rabbit and Mr. Sedberry, seated on either side of me, leaned in to whisper, "We're scared to death." Neither enjoyed public speaking.

When I first arrived at the reunion, I noticed some resentment from the other players. After the roundtable discussion, though, a few approached me.

"That was a great story," they agreed. They warmed up, joking with me and asking me questions.

The program stated, "These living legends will be available for autographs following the event." We were directed to the museum's large rotunda where long tables were stacked with crates of baseballs. The outside doors opened and in tumbled hundreds of children.

I had never autographed a baseball before. To my surprise, I discovered it's not easy to do. Because a ball is round, not flat, it's hard to hold with your left hand and sign with your right. We signed hundreds of baseballs, and when we ran out, we signed their T-shirts, caps, or whatever scrap of papers they had with them. A number of adults got in line, too.

After the last children ran happily out the door with their pieces of history, we were tired. We agreed it was one of the most rewarding days of our lives as we traveled back to Jacksboro. We also laughed that all of our autographs would be worn off that weekend in sandlots all over Dallas. I think that's a much better use of them than gathering dust on a shelf.

What little fame we achieved as Stars faded as quickly as those autographs would, but not our memories of those two seasons together, our friendships, and the happy children in Dallas.

I've always loved children, and in a flash my own children, Jay, Sue, and Clint, have grown up. They had fun and played the games they loved, and that is the most a parent can ask for.

While Jay was attending North Texas State University in Denton, he called to tell me he was walking on the baseball team. I was a little skeptical.

"Jay," I said. "You haven't played ball since Little League."

"I know, Dad, but I think I'd really enjoy it," he said.

I went to his first game against Tarleton State in Stephenville on a lovely spring afternoon. To my great surprise, Jay was the starting pitcher. He wasn't a great pitcher, but he lettered and had a wonderful time. Jay graduated from the University of Maryland, and then obtained his MBA in finance from North Texas University in Denton. He now lives in St. Croix, Virgin Islands, with his wife, Sanni, and daughter, Emma Louise.

Sue, my middle child, graduated from Texas Tech with a double major in journalism and Spanish. She soon moved up the corporate ladder in Austin to become the a vice president in commercial marketing with JP Morgan/Chase. There she met and married cattle buyer and broker Rockland McMahan, and they have two lovely children, Jeremy and Mabrie.

My youngest, Clint Creighton Craft, graduated from Jacksboro High, where he was a linebacker/center and received a scholarship to play Division I college football for the University of the Pacific at Stockton, California, which was at that time part of the Pacific Coast Conference. At the end of his freshman year, he joined the Marine Corps and served in the first Gulf War and in the Somalia conflict.

To our surprise he announced he'd seen enough of the world and, upon discharge, returned to Texas. He lettered in football at Tarleton State University, graduated with a degree in criminal justice, and played linebacker on a minor-league football team, the Azle Avengers. Later he started his own bail bond business and lives on the family ranch north of Jacksboro with his wife, Nadine. His daughter, Hannah, is enrolled at the University of Arkansas.

While I was once busiest with baseball, then my children, and later politics, my family has again become the most important part of my life. It's been amazing to me how my priorities have changed. I met Pamela when she was the administrative assistant of probation for Jack and Wise counties. Our first date was to Jacksboro's homecoming football game in the fall of 1996. We dated for six years, both leery of remarrying. In fact, she suggested marriage first, but I told her I did not intend to remarry. Six months later, I was ready, and then she was not convinced. We finally agreed on May 25, 2002, and we were married in Jacksboro's First United Methodist Church by the Reverend Eric Rothe and by our dear friend, Jack County Judge Mitchell Davenport.

While my time in ranching, cable television, politics, and banking opened new worlds to me, my early years with the Stars had a major influence on who I am today. I hope that others will learn a little bit about baseball and a little bit about life from my story.

REFERENCES

Bragan, Bobby, and Jeff Guinn. 1992. *You Can't Hit the Ball with the Bat on Your Shoulder: The Baseball Life and Times of Bobby Bragan.* Fort Worth: The Summit Group.

Cottrell, R. C. 2001. "Review of John B. Holway's *The Complete Book of Baseball's Negro Leagues: The Other Half of Baseball History.*" *Library Journal* 126 (9): 73.

Craft, Jerry. 1999. Unpublished interview by Mary Nell Westbrook. Jacksboro, Texas. January 24.

The Daily Toreador. 1956. "Extra! Finally! Tech Makes SWC, Tech Breaks SWC Jinx." May 12.

Dallas Star Post. 1959. "Dallas Road Runners 12–1." May 16.

Fink, Robert. 2007. "Semi-Professional African American Baseball in Texas before the Great Depression." *The African American Experience in Texas: An Anthology.* Ed. Bruce A. Glasrud and James M. Smallwood, 218–29. Lubbock: Texas Tech University Press.

References

Gerlach, Larry R. 1998. "Baseball's Other 'Great Experiment': Eddie Klep and the Integration of the Negro Leagues." *Journal of Sport History* (Fall): 453–81.

Henderson, Monroe. 2007. Interview by Kathleen Sullivan. Fort Worth, Texas. July 31.

Holaday, Chris, and Mark Presswood. 2004. *Baseball in Dallas.* Chicago: Arcadia.

Holmes, John. 1984. *Texas Sport: The Illustrated History.* Austin: Texas Monthly Press.

Holway, John B. 2001. *The Complete Book of Baseball's Negro Leagues: The Other Half of Baseball History.* Winter Park, FL: Hastings House.

Horton, Thomas F. 1975. *The History of Jack County.* Fort Worth: J. Robert Dennis.

Huckaby, Ida Laster. 1949. *Ninety-Four Years in Jack County: 1854–1948.* Austin: Steck.

Jack County Genealogical Society. 1985. *The History of Jack County.* Dallas: Curtis Media Corp.

Myles, Clarence "Rabbit." 2007. Interview by Kathleen Sullivan. Wichita Falls, Texas. February 17.

Myles, Clarence "Rabbit." 1999. Unpublished interview by Mary Nell Westbrook. Graham, Texas. March 3.

Peterson, Robert. 1970. *Only the Ball Was White: A History of Legendary Black Players and All-Black Professional Teams.* New York: Gramercy Books.

Powers, Ned. 1959. "The Negro Leagues/The Cuban Connection." *Saskatoon Star Phoenix.* Augus22. www.attheplate.com/wcbl/negro2.htm.

Presswood, Mark, and Chris Holaday. 2004. *Baseball in Fort Worth.* Chicago: Arcadia.

Rampersad, Arnold. 1997. *Jackie Robinson: A Biography.* New York: Ballantine.

Sedberry, Carl. 1999. Unpublished interview by Mary Nell Westbrook. Graham, Texas. March 3.

Snyder, Brad. 2004. *Beyond the Shadow of the Senators: The Untold Story of the Homestead Grays and the Integration of Baseball.* New York: McGraw-Hill.

INDEX